Berger

Financial Innovations in International Debt Management

(Fortsetzung am Ende des Buches)

Walter Berger

Financial Innovations in International Debt Management

An Institutional Analysis

GABLER

CIP-Titelaufnahme der Deutschen Bibliothek

Berger, Walter:
Financial innovations in international debt management : an institutional analysis / Walter Berger. – Wiesbaden : Gabler, 1990
(Neue betriebswirtschaftliche Forschung ; 73)
Zugl. : Konstanz, Univ., Diss., 1990

NE: GT

ISBN-13: 978-3-409-13733-1 e-ISBN-13: 978-3-322-89330-7
DOI: 10.1007/978-3-322-89330-7

Der Gabler Verlag ist ein Unternehmen der Verlagsgruppe Bertelsmann International.

Lektorat: Jutta Hauser-Fahr

PREFACE

The international debt problem has already generated a huge number of publications. Why then another publication? Many publications address macroeconomic implications of the debt problem, others investigate special new financing instruments such as debt equity swaps, others discuss the economic or legal aspects of debt reschedulings. This work of Walter Berger concentrates on the evolution of the financial side of the debt problem. This evolution is fascinating since it reveals a continuous expansion of the financial instruments being used and a surprising change in intercreditor relationships. While in the seventies equal treatment of creditors was not of much concern, this changed dramatically in the eighties. But lately equal treatment turned out to be a strong impediment to the creditors' management of loan portfolios. Hence, inequality of treatment is growing again. This development represents a challenge to everyone who tries to explain legal changes by using economic theory.

Another characteristic of Walter Berger's work is that he starts from a broad institutional perspective. Most economists analyze the debt problem by assuming a world where everybody follows the same principles of rationality and optimization. Walter Berger questions this approach by arguing that cultural discrepancies among creditor countries and indebted countries make it difficult to define efficiency by "Western" standards only. Moreover, different cultures create what Berger calls "institutional obfuscation", that is, creditors have substantial difficulties to predict the behavior of differently minded debtors, and vice versa. This lack of information creates a transaction risk for each contracting party. Thus, Berger warns us to derive solutions of the debt problem starting only from Western paradigms. It is difficult to predict the success of financial innovations which require the collaboration of creditors and a differently minded debtor.

Walter Berger concentrates on the creditors' objectives when he analyzes efficiency gains from financial innovations. Efficiency gains are measured as reductions of transaction costs. Berger uses a fine taxonomy of transaction costs to discuss efficiency gains. One important aspect is that contract enforcement costs primarily serve to reduce transaction risks. Hence, financial innovations also have to be analyzed with respect to their impact on transaction risks. This aspect has been ignored so far in the literature.

As the creditors' behavior depends also on the institutional environment of their domicile countries, Berger illustrates this by comparing taxation and bank regulation in two important creditor countries, the United States of America and the Federal Republic of Germany. Tax and regulatory arbitrage are two important motives for creditors to shift claims across borders and, thus, cannot be ignored when analyzing innovations that facilitate the trading of rescheduling country loans.

Although every economic explanation of success or failure of financial innovations necessarily contains speculative elements, this work of Walter Berger reveals many new insights into the evolution of the financing side of the international debt problem and, thus, should help us to understand this evolution much better.

GÜNTER FRANKE

ACKNOWLEDGEMENTS

No research, let alone knowledge is possible without the possibility to communicate. There has been a great number of people that have been willing to share their opinion and knowledge with me or have contributed to my ability to understand and progress in the course of my work. I want to thank them although I cannot mention all of them.

I had the opportunity of many constructive conversations with my colleagues from the Law Department of the Universität Konstanz, in particular Ulrich Messer, Thomas Roth, and Jörg Wulfken. I thank them for their support and the insight they helped me to gain into the legal ramifications of my subject. Also to Christian Harm, New York University, and Jack Wahl, Institute of International Financial Management at the Universität Konstanz, who have been patient discussants, I owe thanks.

An important influence on my work stems from two stays in Washington, D.C. I benefited substantially from a research internship with the Institute of International Finance (IIF) and a visiting scholarship with the International Law Institute (ILI) that both provided me with an organizational base to conduct my research. Especially John Haseltine and Jack Ross have been very helpful during this time in which I developed a sense of the political complexity of international lending.

I want to thank my supervisor Professor Günter Franke for his support and advice during the various stages of my work and Professor Carsten Thomas Ebenroth for taking on the role as second referee for my dissertation. Last but not least I thank the Deutsche Forschungsgemeinschaft (DFG) for the financial support I received through the special research program (SFB) 178 "Internationalisierung der Wirtschaft" at the Universität Konstanz.

WALTER BERGER

TABLE OF CONTENTS

ABBREVIATIONS XIII

LIST OF FIGURES AND TABLES XV

1. INTRODUCTION 1
   1.1. Subject and Purpose of Inquiry 1
   1.2. Course of Inquiry 4

2. AN ANALYTICAL FRAMEWORK FOR AN EFFICIENCY ASSESSMENT OF INNOVATIONS IN INTERNATIONAL DEBT MANAGEMENT 6
   2.1. Terminological and Conceptual Prolegomena 6
      2.1.1. Institutions and Financial Culture 6
      2.1.2. Innovation 10
      2.1.3. The Relationship Between Institutions and the Concept of Efficiency 11
   2.2. Transaction Costs 18
      2.2.1. Origin of the Transaction Cost Approach 18
      2.2.2. Methodological Implications 20
      2.2.3. A Taxonomy of Transaction Costs 23
   2.3. Causes for the Emergence of Transaction Costs in International Debt Management 27
      2.3.1. Obstacles for the Enforcement of International Loan Contracts 27
      2.3.2. Examples of Enforcement Cost Inducing Behavior 29
         2.3.2.1. Capital Flight 30
         2.3.2.2. Corruption 31
         2.3.2.3. Free Rider Behavior 32
         2.3.2.4. Herding 33
   2.4. Transaction Risks 34
      2.4.1. A Taxonomy of Transaction Risks 35
      2.4.2. Risk Management 38
   2.5. Summary 39

3. THE EVOLUTION OF INNOVATIONS IN INTERNATIONAL DEBT MANAGEMENT....41
3.1. The International Debt Crisis....41
3.1.1. Economic Background....41
3.1.2. The "Baker Plan"....43
3.1.3. The "Brady Plan"....44
3.1.4. Three Stages of Debt Crisis Management....45
3.1.5. The Menu Approach....47
3.2. Institutional Background of Innovations in International Debt Management....49
3.2.1. The Syndication Mechanism....49
3.2.2. Specifics of the Rescheduling Process....50
3.2.3. Important Contractual Provisions....54
3.2.3.1. Cross Default Clause....55
3.2.3.2. Pari Passu Clause....56
3.2.3.3. Negative Pledge Clause....57
3.2.3.4. Sharing Clause....57
3.2.3.5. Mandatory Prepayment Clause....57
3.2.3.6. Other Clauses....58
3.3. Recent Innovations....59
3.3.1. The Secondary Market for Rescheduling Country Debt....59
3.3.1.1. Participants....59
3.3.1.2. Transaction Modes....60
3.3.1.3. Legal Institutions....60
3.3.1.3.1. Novation....61
3.3.1.3.2. Assignment....61
3.3.1.3.3. Participation....62
3.3.1.4. Volume and Pricing....62
3.3.2. Debt Reduction Modes....65
3.3.2.1. Debt Equity Swaps....66
3.3.2.2. Debt for Debt Swaps....67
3.3.2.3. Debt Buy-Backs....68
3.3.2.4. Debt for Nature Swaps....69
3.3.2.5. Debt for Development Swaps....69
3.3.2.6. Debt for Commodity Swaps....70

4. INSTITUTIONAL DETERMINANTS OF INNOVATIONS IN INTERNATIONAL DEBT MANAGEMENT ... 71
4.1. Sector-Specific Regulatory Determinants in the United States of America ... 72
4.1.1. Supervisory Determinants ... 72
4.1.1.1. Reporting Requirements ... 73
4.1.1.2. Capital Requirements ... 74
4.1.1.3. Lending Limits ... 76
4.1.1.4. Loan Classification Requirements ... 76
4.1.1.5. Reserve Requirements ... 78
4.1.1.6. Accounting for Fees ... 81
4.1.1.7. The Ninety-Day-Rule ... 81
4.1.1.8. Debt Equity Swap Regulation ... 82
4.1.2. Tax-related Determinants ... 84
4.1.2.1. Reserves ... 84
4.1.2.2. Debt Reduction Modes ... 85
4.1.2.3. Foreign Tax Credit Determination ... 86
4.1.2.4. Charitable Contributions ... 88
4.1.3. Accounting Determinants ... 89
4.1.3.1. Reserves ... 90
4.1.3.2. "Troubled Debt Restructurings" ... 92
4.1.3.3. Secondary Market Transactions ... 94
4.1.3.4. Debt Equity Swaps ... 95
4.1.3.5. Debt for Debt Swaps ... 97
4.1.3.6. Debt for Nature Swaps ... 98
4.2. Sector-Specific Regulatory Determinants in the Federal Republic of Germany ... 99
4.2.1. Supervisory Determinants ... 99
4.2.1.1. Reporting Requirements ... 99
4.2.1.2. Reserve Requirements ... 101
4.2.1.3. Capital Requirements ... 103
4.2.1.4. Lending Limits ... 104
4.2.1.5. Debt Equity Swap Regulation ... 104
4.2.2. Tax-related Determinants ... 104
4.2.3. Accounting Determinants ... 106

4.3. Comparison ... 107
4.4. Firm-Specific Determinants ... 111
4.4.1. Strategy and Organization ... 112
4.4.2. Financial Policy ... 113
4.5. International Political Determinants ... 116
4.5.1. Foreign Policy Considerations of Domicile Countries ... 116
4.5.2. Debtor Country Sovereignty Violation ... 117

5. EFFICIENCY ANALYSIS OF INNOVATIONS IN INTERNATIONAL DEBT MANAGEMENT ... 121
5.1. Secondary Market Transactions ... 121
5.1.1. Reduction of Transaction Risks ... 121
5.1.2. Reduction of Transaction Costs ... 122
5.1.2.1. The Creditor Bank's Perspective ... 122
5.1.2.2. The Rescheduling Country's Perspective ... 127
5.1.3. Comparative Analysis of Debt Transfer Modes ... 128
5.1.4. Obstacles for Further Efficiency Gains ... 130
5.2. Debt Equity Swaps ... 131
5.2.1. The Creditor Bank's Perspective ... 132
5.2.2. The Investor's Perspective ... 135
5.2.3. The Rescheduling Country's Perspective ... 135
5.2.4. Obstacles for Further Efficiency Gains ... 136
5.3. Other Debt Reduction Modes ... 138
5.3.1. Debt for Debt Swaps ... 138
5.3.2. Debt Buy-Backs ... 140
5.3.3. Debt for Nature and Debt for Development Swaps ... 142
5.3.4. Debt for Commodity Swaps ... 143
5.4. Summary ... 144

6. CONCLUSIONS ... 146

REFERENCES ... 149

ABBREVIATIONS

Abs.	Absatz
AICPA	American Institute of Certified Public Accountants
AktG	Aktiengesetz
Aufl.	Aufl.
ATRR	Allocated Transfer Risk Reserve
BAK	Bundesaufsichtsamt für das Kreditwesen
BAnz	Bundesanzeiger
Bd.	Band
BHC	Bank Holding Company
BHCA	Bank Holding Company Act
BFH	Bundesfinanzhof
BFHE	Bundesfinanzhofentscheidungen
BIZ	Bank für Internationalen Zahlungsausgleich
bn.	billion
cf.	confer
CFR	Code of Federal Regulations
OCC	Office of the Comptroller of the Currency
DAC	Development Assistance Committee
DHIRSA	Domestic Housing and International Recovery and Stability Act
ed., eds.	edition or editor, editors
e.g.	example given
ENPV	Expected Net Present Value
FASB	Financial Accounting Standards Board
FDIC	Federal Deposit Insurance Corporation
FFIEC	Federal Financial Institutions Examination Council
f.i.	for instance
FRB	Board of Governors of the Federal Reserve System
GAAP	Generally Accepted Accounting Standards
H.	Heft
HGB	Handelsgesetzbuch
Hrsg.	Herausgeber
IADB	Inter-American Development Bank
ibid.	ibidem
ICERC	Interagency Country Exposure Review Committee
i.e.	id est
IFC	International Finance Corporation
IFR	International Financing Review
ILSA	International Lending Supervision Act
IMF	International Monetary Fund
IRC	Internal Revenue Code
IRS	Internal Revenue Service
Jg.	Jahrgang
KWG	Kreditwesengesetz
LDC	Less Developed Country
LIBOR	London Interbank Offered Rate
m.	million
MIGA	Multilateral Investment Guarantee Agency
n.	note
n.a.	not applicable

No.	Number
Nr.	Nummer
ODC	Overseas Development Council
OECD	Organization for Economic Cooperation and Development
OPEC	Organization of Petroleum Exporting Countries
OTRP	Other Transfer Risk Problems
p.	page
PB	Practice Buletin
resp.	respectively
SAB	Staff Accounting Bulletin
SEC	Security Exchange Commission
SFAC	Statement of Financial Accounting Concepts
SFAS	Statement of Financial Accounting Standards
seq., seqq.	sequens, sequentes
TRA	Tax Reform Act
US, U.S.	United States
USA	United States of America
US$	US-American Dollar
U.S.C.	United States Code
U.S.C.A.	United States Code Annotated
v.	vide
v.	vom
Vol., Vols.	Volume, Volumes
v.s.	vide supra
Ziff.	Ziffer

LIST OF FIGURES AND TABLES

FIGURES:

Figure 1: Institutional Elements of Financial Culture......9
Figure 2: A Stylized Hierarchy of Social Institutions and Objectives......15
Figure 3: Transaction Cost Categories......25
Figure 4: Secondary Market Pricing of Rescheduling Country Loans, January 1988-September 1989......63

TABLES:

Table 1: Total External Debt of Less-Industrialized Countries 1982-1990 (US$ billion)......2
Table 2: Foreign Borrowing by Less-Industrialized Countries from Private Creditors 1970-1985......42
Table 3: Elements of the Menu of Options Used by Commercial Banks...48
Table 4: Multilateral Debt Rescheduling Agreements with Commercial Banks 1982-1989......53
Table 5: Rescheduling Country Debt Conversions 1984-1986......65
Table 6: Volume of Debt Equity Swap Transactions in Selected Debtor Countries......67
Table 7: US Banks' Claims on Selected Rescheduling Countries 1982-1988......72
Table 8: Developing-Country Exposure and Loan-Loss Coverage of large U.S. Banks at Year-end 1987......79
Table 9: Reserve Rates Required by ICERC......81
Table 10: Standard Income-Statement Format......90
Table 11: Standard Balance-Sheet Format......92
Table 12: German Banks' (domestic domicile, foreign branches, and foreign subsidiaries of German banks) Claims on Selected Rescheduling Countries......100
Table 13: Indicative Country Risk Reserve Levels with German Banks...103
Table 14: Comparison of Supervisory, Tax and Accounting Institutions in the USA and Germany......108

Table 15: Comparison of Regulations on Commercial Bank Provisioning against Rescheduling Countries in Selected Industrial Countries at End-1987 111
Table 16: Ratios of Rescheduling Country Loans to Total Loans at Selected US-Banks 123

1. INTRODUCTION

1.1. SUBJECT AND PURPOSE OF INQUIRY

The so-called international[1] debt crisis now lasts since the Mexican announcement not to continue service on its external debt in August 1982. As is illustrated by table 1, the total amount of external debt of less-industrialized countries[2] increased from US$ 839 billion in 1982 to an estimated US$ 1319 billion in 1990. Many of these countries experienced payment problems and underwent reschedulings of their foreign debt. Almost two thirds of the debt of the severely indebted middle income countries in this period has been owed to private commercial banks (cf. table 1).

Progress in international debt management has been perceived to be rather slowly forthcoming. A fundamental obstacle for arriving at adequate policies is its multidisciplinary reach. It pervades problems associated with political and economic organization, international law, cultural diversity, ethical postulates, private business interests, social equality, and - perceived more recently - ecological consequences.

---

1 This term is used in a very broad sense. It characterizes all phenomena that involve at least two nations, jurisdictions or currencies. It often also extends to cultures although, for such cases, "intercultural" would be the more appropriate term .

2 The use of the term "developing country" will be avoided wherever possible. Two implications of this term appear to make its use inappropriate for the context in which it is most often used. The first implication lies in its distinction from "industrialized country" which suggests that these do not develop or may at least have no need for development. In fact, in terms of industrial structure or econonomic growth "industrialized countries" often develop faster than "less-industrialized countries". The second implication is more fundamental as it suggests the existence of a need of development, the perception of which may or may not exist. The term "less-industrialized country" will be used instead. In addition the terms "rescheduling country" and "debtor country" will be used interchangeably as they reflect much more closely the phenomena investigated here.

Literature dealing with reasons, analysis, interpretation and potential "solutions" of the debt crisis is overwhelmingly extensive[3]. This study does not indulge in reinvestigating proposals forwarded to "solve" the debt crisis, nor is it intended to add another "new" proposal to that list. Rather, its purpose shall be to identify the causes for the emergence of a set of innovative transaction modes in the course of the debt management process that are perceived to have led to efficiency improvements in credit relationships between rescheduling countries and private commercial banks.

Table 1: Total External Debt of Less-Industrialized Countries 1982-1990 (US$ billion)

Category	1982	1983	1984	1985	1986	1987	1988[a]	1989[b]	1990[c]
All countries	**839**	**905**	**936**	**1041**	**1146**	**1292**	**1284**	**1290**	**1319**
DRS countries[d]	**753**	**819**	**855**	**952**	**1047**	**1176**	**1156**	**1165**	**1189**
Long-term debt[e]	561	644	684	780	882	999	980	995	1039
Owed to banks[f]	283	335	363	375	398	418	396	n.a.	n.a.
Percent	50%	50%	53%	48%	45%	42%	40%	n.a.	n.a.
SIMI countries[g]	**382**	**408**	**426**	**457**	**486**	**536**	**516**	**518**	**n.a.**
Long-term debt[e]	272	324	349	384	423	463	441	442	n.a.
Owed to banks[f]	187	226	248	251	268	278	255	n.a.	n.a.
Percent	69%	70%	71%	65%	63%	60%	58%	n.a.	n.a.

----
[a] - Estimates.
[b] - Preliminary estimates.
[c] - Projections.
[d] - 111 less-industrialized countries that report to the World Bank Debtor Reporting System.
[e] - Debt with original or extended maturity of more than one year.
[f] - Long-term debt owed to commercial banks.
[g] - "Severely Indebted Middle Income Countries": Argentina, Bolivia, Brazil, Chile, Congo, Costa Rica, Cote d'Ivoire, Ecuador, Honduras, Hungary, Mexico, Morocco, Nicaragua, Peru, Philippines, Poland, Senegal, Uruguay, Venezuela. These are countries in which three of the following four ratios fall in the specified ranges: debt to GNP (30-50%), debt to exports of goods and all services (165-275%), accrued debt service to exports (18-30%), and accrued interest to exports (12-20%).

Source: *World Bank* [1989b].

---

3 For a short account of the broad range of perceived reasons for the debt crisis cf. *Holtz* [1988, 13seqq.]. For overviews of proposals for "solutions" v. *Kettell/Magnus* [1986, 163seqq.] and *Wertman* [1987].

Hence, the subject of the study is a set of product innovations that are in some way based on the valuation of commercial bank loans to rescheduling countries in a secondary market. In the absence of an international bankruptcy code that could provide for the enforcement of these claims the secondary market emerged as the most important organizational innovation in the course of the debt crisis. The innovations in question either involve an actual secondary market transaction (market-based) or emulate secondary market pricing through negotiated conversion conditions (market-related).

An underlying premise of the following analysis is that it is a unique complex of sector- and individual firm-specific institutional factors which accounts for the behavior of banks in deciding on the most adequate, i.e. efficient, transaction modes and, thus, its economic consequences. This complex consists both of institutional prescriptions for behavior inside and outside the stipulations of the underlying contractual relationship.

A consideration of this complex of institutional factors is also important in designing appropriate policies in dealing with the debt crisis both for individual banks and for governments. The distinction that is often made between economic and institutional (or political, regulatory etc.) factors (cf. *Friesen* [1986, 2]) blurrs the institutional foundations of any economic organization. For instance, *Dale* [1984, 1] characterizes multinational banking as distinct from international banking as "*... an artifice born of regulatory anomalies*".

Therefore some emphasis will be given to the relationships between banks and their regulatory organizations. Innovations in banks' relationships with rescheduling countries will be analyzed primarily from the perspective of individual banks. This analysis shall provide an explanation for the difference of banks' tactics and innovative actions in muddling through a hitherto "successfull" international debt management process.

Conceptually, the analysis is based on a transaction cost approach specifically tailored to long-term international credit transactions. Transaction costs are perceived as a consequence of the institutional prescriptions for engaging in transactions. These institutions determine the subjective perception of advantages and/or costs of onc institutional arrangement relative to another. In other words, the evolutionary process of institutional innovation is viewed to be driven by the search for transaction cost advantages within particular institutional settings. In this context the study also serves as a contribution to the discussion of the scope and possible content of a theory of economic institutions, the transaction cost approach in general, and, in the widest sense, organization theory.

1.2. COURSE OF INQUIRY

The ensuing chapter sets the conceptual delineations for the study, provides definitions, and briefly discusses some methodological aspects. The central theoretical concept which contains the definition of the applicable efficiency criteria to be applied in later chapters - primarily in chapter 5 - is presented. The next chapter provides an overview over the evolution and the elements of debt crisis management. It covers important institutional background considerations, i.e. in particular the most relevant contractual provisions, and describes the innovations in question.

Chapter 4 consists of an analysis of selected institutional determinants for banks' decisions concerning rescheduling country loans. The emphasis is on regulatory determinants - namely supervisory, tax, and accounting concerns -, particularly in the USA as the most relevant sector-specific determinants. These institutions are subject to continuous change by law makers and other actors of the financial sector. Therefore, this analysis can only be of an exemplary character. For comparative purposes the respective German[4] regulations are described as well. An examination of other jurisdictions would have been beyond the scope of the study's purpose. In addition, two other bank-external determinants - foreign policy considerations and the problem of debtor country sovereignty violation - and firm-specific determinants are considered briefly.

---

[4] Here, the term German always refers to the Federal Republic of Germany.

Both, chapters 3 and 4 cannot claim to provide a comprehensive treatment of all relevant institutional determinants; the selection is based on perceived importance. In chapter 5 the existence of the innovations presented in chapter 3 is explained by applying the criteria introduced in chapter 2. I.e. it is discussed in which way these innovative transaction modes help the associated parties to economize on transaction costs. Concluding remarks are added in the final chapter.

2. AN ANALYTICAL FRAMEWORK FOR AN EFFICIENCY ASSESSMENT OF INNOVATIONS IN DEBT CRISIS MANAGEMENT

Overviews of the various approaches economic scientists have tried to use for explaining phenomena related to international credit relationships have been offered by *Darity/Horn* [1988], *Eaton/Taylor* [1986], *Glick* [1986], and *Taylor* [1985]. The approach chosen here is intended to be in line with what could be called the move from financial economics to institutional finance. It is a basic premise of the following deliberations that without an analysis of the most relevant institutional conditions for international commercial bank lending a large part of the innovative transaction modes that emerged in the course of debt crisis management cannot be explained. This contention shall therefore be based on the "*growing agreement* (in financial economics; author's note) *that institutions matter in ways not hitherto acknowledged or even imagined.*" (*Williamson* [1988, 587]).

2.1. TERMINOLOGICAL AND CONCEPTUAL PROLEGOMENA

2.1.1. Institutions and Financial Culture

For the purposes of this study institutions are defined as rules or norms of behavior that represent or form part of a regular pattern of a (financial) transaction (in short: transaction mode). Fundamentally, a transaction is a separable set of goal-oriented, i.e. purposeful actions. Here, a transaction shall be understood as a separable set of actions that effects the perceived distribution of property rights among participating actors[5].

Institutions are a multifaceted research object for the social sciences. It is impossible here even to summarize the many attempts to describe and explain their nature and function. The fundamental role institutions play in the study of social phenomena is evident from the axiomatic distinction generally made between two extreme alternative views of the role of institutions. One is that

---

5 Following *Furubotn/Pejovich* [1974, 3], "*Property rights are understood as the sanctioned behavioral relations among men that arise from the existence of goods and pertain to their use*".

institutions determine the way individual actors design their relationships with other actors. The other is that individual actors create institutions in order to design their relationships with other actors.

Mainstream economics has for the major part of this century treated institutions, i.e. in particular legal institutions, as exogenously given data. Thus, it has mostly avoided to consider the mutual feedback between individual actors or groups of actors as designers of institutions and institutions as designers of actors' actions[6]. The entire set of all institutions relevant for all conceivable actions of individual actors or groups of actors is defined here as their culture. Hence, culture can at the same time be viewed as the set of all determinants of actors' actions and as the product of actors' actions.

Institutional determinants relevant for the analysis of international credit relationships are innumerable. Most apparent are the institutional determinants contained in the underlying contracts, e.g. their various clauses, which specify a certain behavior for the contracting parties. However, experience has shown that further institutional determinants such as regulatory and tax laws along with certain accounting practices also have a significant influence on the behavior of banks in the debt management process (cf. *Friesen* [1986], *Dale* [1984]), and *Link* [1984]. In addition, firm-specific and financial sector-specific organizational and procedural conditions as well as foreign policy ramifications are other important determinants of banks' country lending and loan trading decisions.

On more elementary levels yet, the institutional elements of national cultural systems, i.e. their traditional values and morals, the ideological foundations of the political system, and the historical evolution of economic organization, in particular of the financial sector, in different cultural environments are reflected in the behavior of banks as they are in the design of laws and regulations relevant for engaging in banking activities (cf. *Arpan/Radebaugh* [1981, 19seqq.]). However,

---

6 Certainly, the second perspective is hard to conceive in an extending "Western" culture pervaded with the concepts of anthropocentrism and organismic individuality. Cf. also *Veljanovski* [1982, 5seqq.] who offers more possible explanations of economists' neglect of the investigation of legal institutions in particular. The conflict implied herein between a "free will" and a "deterministic" perspective of the impact of institutions on behavior cannot be elaborated upon.

this study puts the emphasis on the investigation of the impact of selected institutions contained in the tax and supervisory laws, accounting conventions and the transaction modes of international credit relationships themselves. Two national "cultures", namely the United States of America and the Federal Republic of Germany (in the following only: Germany), will serve as examples.

Financial transactions are governed by the set of institutions relevant for the behavior of actors within the financial sector - in other words the system of behavioral rules for people working for or with financial firms[7], e.g. banks. Four categories of such institutions can be distinguished. These categories constitute what is called here "financial culture" (figure 1). The denominations for these categories, namely regulations, organizations, processes, and products, are only intended to provide a terminological structure for institutions of different character.

Two further distinctions are made. The first one differentiates sector-specific from firm-specific institutions. Sector-specific institutions affect the design of transactions while being independent from the activities of an individual firm. On the other hand, firm-specific institutions impact the design of transactions as effected by individual firms. The second distinction refers to the origin of the institutions in question. Legal institutions are designed by lawmakers. Non-legal institutions are designed by all other participants of the financial sector, i.e. in particular financial firms, or have evolved from their actions.

---

7 Here, the term "financial institution" is not used in order to avoid confusion. This use of the term "institution" can be attributed to the "corporate body" interpretation - the second broad category of definitions of the term "institution" (cf. *Vanberg* [1983, 55seq.]). The definition used for this study belongs into the "social norms" - category of definitions. However, as soon as one takes into account that the stability of any corporate body again depends on the stability of social norms, it becomes evident that any corporate body can be interpreted as a complex of social norms, i.e. institutions. The distinction that *Vanberg* draws when he characterizes corporate bodies as intended for organized, planned, coordinated action and social norms as principally unintentional does not reflect the requirement that purposeful action is only possible on the basis of institutionalized norms. Also, both interpretations have in common the expression of a need of mutual adaptation between individuals or groups of individuals (*ibid.* [57, 62]).

Figure 1: Institutional Elements of Financial Culture[a]

FINANCIAL CULTURE
(Perspective of individual firm)

REGULATIONS		ORGANIZATIONS		PROCESSES		PRODUCTS	
Sector-specific	Firm-specific	Sector-specific	Firm-specific	Sector-specific	Firm-specific	Sector-specific	Firm-specific
Legal Supervisory laws Tax laws Accounting Rules		**Legal** Laws specifying a particular economic organization	**Legal** Laws of incor-poration By-laws and statutes	**Legal** Bankruptcy procedures		**Legal** Forms of contracts (i.e. general format of loan contract)	**Legal** Contracts for specific services (e.g. individual loan contract)
Non-legal Accounting Rules General Business Practices Business ethics	**Non-legal** Business objectives and strategy Stated principles of corporate culture	**Non-legal** Hierarchies Markets Cartels	**Non-legal** Divisional and matrix organizations Profit centers Joint ventures Incentive systems	**Non-legal** Rescheduling procedures Trading procedures	**Non-legal** Decision-making procedures, e.g. (Country) risk analysis Planning processes Asset and liability management Behavioral impacts of technologies	**Non-legal** Syndicated Euroloans (concept) Debt equity swaps (concept)	**Non-legal** Syndicated Euroloans (actual design) Debt equity swaps (actual design)

Feedback relationships

[a] Examples chosen represent a selection only.

These definitions are chosen purely for the purpose of this study. The definitions and examples as contained in figure 1 are certainly not exhaustive. For other purposes other definitions and examples may be more appropriate. It is also unavoidable that certain overlapping may occur among various delineations of institutions.

Besides providing a terminological framework, the figure is also intended to illustrate the mutual feedback between effects of many different institutions of legal and non-legal nature. This is of particular relevance in designing new institutions like new financial instruments. For example, debt equity swaps emerged both as a response to cost considerations of creditor banks as well as from the availability of legal rules designed by rescheduling country law-makers[8]. On the other hand, US law has been changed in order to enable increased use of debt equity swaps.

Another important message lies in pointing out that both sector-specific or other firm-external and firm-specific or firm-internal[9] institutions are relevant for an explanation of behavior. This point is considered important as in the course of further analysis a main tenet of organizational theory may fade out of sight, i.e. that behavior <u>of</u> firms is always behavior <u>in</u> firms.

2.1.2. Innovation

The perception of increasing complexity of financial transaction modes in the recent past made the term (financial) "innovation" a buzzword. Here, a financial innovation (in the following only: innovation) shall simply be understood as any financial transaction mode or change in the combination of structural elements of a financial transaction mode that is perceived to be new and beneficial. Transaction modes in this context may comprise individual financial instruments, markets and other conduit mechanisms for money. "New and beneficial" can be

---

8 For a description of debt equity swaps v. section 3.3.2.1.

9 For a general exposé of the function of firm-internal institutions in the sense of behavioral norms within firms v. *Drumm* [1990, 574seq.]

understood much in the same way as *Miller*'s [1986, 460][10] statistically based definition of innovations as unforecastable improvements. This definition would for example comprise any new trading mechanism, any new contractual clause or covenant, or any new linkage of contractual terms to certain conditions etc. which the participating parties deem beneficial[11].

This very general notion of innovation is at the root of cultural change, i.e the evolution of cultures (cf. *Hayek* [1973, 13]) - in this specific context of financial culture. Institutions emerge from originally innovative transactions as eventually established future rules of conduct. This does not mean that experience and theorizing do not play a role in "inventing" innovative transaction modes. But the success or perceived relative benefit - based upon criteria believed to indicate improvements in survival potential[12] - of an innovation can never be completely ascertained ex ante. Only after the first test of a new transaction mode can it or elements of it be called an innovation because it successfully enabled an intended transaction.

2.1.3. The Relationship between Institutions and the Concept of Efficiency

The emergence of innovations in the sense defined above implies a perceived improvement of efficiency. Thus, in order to explain innovations, the relevant subjectively perceived efficiency criteria have to be identified. Due to the complexity of international credit relationships it is difficult to establish general criteria for the identification of efficiency gains. Such criteria should be

---

10 *"For the term "innovation" and how it differs from just plain improvement, modern statistics provide some helpful distinctions. Time-series analysts break into two parts the change over time in the value of any series such as the Gross National Product or consumer prices. One part is the change that could, in principle at least, have been forecasted by extrapolating known past information. The other part is thus the unanticipated, unforecastable change, the "surprise", as it were. It is these surprises that have been aptly dubbed the "innovations" in the time series. And it is to their counterparts among the recent surge of financial instruments and institutions that I will be directing attention."* (*Miller* [1986, 460]).

11 For surveys of recent financial innovations cf. *BIS* [1986] and *Ebenroth* [1989].

12 The criteria applied in this study are presented in sections 2.2. to 2.4.

operational in the sense that they account for the influence of many institutional determinants relevant for participating actors.

When dealing with the notion of efficiency, economists usually start from allocative or "economic"[13] efficiency in the Paretian sense. In order to evaluate the efficiency of institutional innovations for managing rescheduling country debt such a concept of efficiency may seem farfetched. There are hardly any other economic exchange relationships that are more obfuscated by political, i.e. supervisory, tax, or foreign and domestic policy influences and conflicting private interests. However, as a point of reference for deriving a concept of efficient contractual arrangements the concept of allocative efficiency is generally considered a useful methodological tool.

In this sense, a contract is efficient when no other contract can be conceived by the contracting parties that would provide an advantage for at least one contracting party without simultaneously causing a disadvantage for at least one other contracting party (*Franke/Hax* [1988, 361])[14]. The problem of determining an efficient contractual design arises with the perception of cost differences between a variety of possible contractual designs when deciding on the participation in a contractual relationship. However, these cost differences are the reflection of cost differences of subjectively perceived feasible courses of action and costs associated with the preparation and enforcement of the associated contract.

---

13 For the problems involved in using this term in this context see *Sen* [1987, 33passim].

14 However, whether one party perceives a disadvantage can only be ascertained by this very party. The other party would not know without prior communication. Hence, for one party to know what contract - or transaction mode based thereon - is more efficient - in the allocative sense - than another one would require complete information about the subjective perception of the expected effects of the contract by the other party. However, given that communication is costly this can never be the case. But allocative efficiency can only yield unequivocal results under conditions of perfect competition. Thus, allocative efficiency can only be used as an ideal transsubjective criterion for allowing an ex ante efficiency assessment of a contract, i.e. it can only be used jointly by all parties. Individual parties will never be completely informed about the objectives of other parties. Ex post, every contract is efficient by definition; otherwise it would not have materialized. V. also the critique of the concept of allocative efficiency by *Sälter* [1989, 122].

In order to attain certain objectives, the parties have to make decisions about a particular course of action from a set of perceived feasible courses of action. The feasibility of courses of action is determined by constraints posed by the unique institutional environments of each individual party relevant for a particular decision. Criteria for choice of an action are derived from individual parties' objectives and are used to decide on a particular transaction and - mutatis mutandis - on a particular contractual design. Again, institutional conditions unique for each party constrain and thereby determine the parties' ability to identify adequate criteria.

From the perspective of any contracting party these subjective pretransactional criteria can be used ex post to determine the "party-efficiency" of a particular result of the action by relating the outcome to the established criteria[15]. If the criteria were not reasonably fitted to the situation they can lead to a misinterpretation of the efficiency analysis. In other words, incentives and restraints created by the institutional setting ex ante can ex post lead to the perception of an institutionally obfuscated, i.e. inefficient contractual relationship from the banks' perspective.

If the kind of institutional determinants relevant for the behavior of party X is unfamiliar to party Y, or if the number of such determinants is very high, they will obfuscate the effects of the institutional determinants contained in the contract on the behavior of party X from the perspective of party Y. This is because, apart from the behavioral prescriptions of the contract itself, such outside institutions

---

15 This, however, is a different concept of efficiency as its purpose is not to assess allocative efficiency but rather deals with the evaluation of deviations from expected outcomes by individual contracting parties. Party-efficiency can serve as a subjective, i.e. party- or firm-specific, measure of the degree of objective attainment through a particular institutional/contractual arrangement. In comparison, allocative efficiency requires the joint consideration of the objectives of all parties. Hence, if banks view international credit relationships with rescheduling countries as inefficient two questions can be asked. Did the banks' actions not meet their efficiency criteria - i.e. did they not act according to their objectives? -, or did their efficiency analysis not meet their efficiency criteria - i.e. did they not measure correctly costs and revenues? The first question concerns the object of measurement; the second question concerns the technique of measurement. From the banks' perspective two answers are possible. First, their efficiency criteria (decision criteria) may have been inadequate. They may have been inappropriate to be applied to lending decisions concerning less-industrialized sovereign states. Second, their efficiency analysis (country risk analysis) may have been inadequate or misinterpreted.

also determine part of the behavior relevant for participating in the contractual relationship, and, thus, for enforcing the contract. This institutional obfuscation of contractually specified behavior tends to be insignificant in transactions within institutional settings that are highly familiar to all contracting parties, like, e.g., in a family. It tends to be greatest in international, or cross-cultural transactions.

Such institutional "imperfections" - that from an opposite perspective could also be termed (cultural) "perfections" of an abstract ideal[16] - are innumerable and only those can be taken into account that are observable and have some kind of perceived dominance over others in the context of international credit relationships. To remove or overcome institutional imperfections or constraints then is customarily viewed as a move towards the ideal, "efficient" situation.

But to reduce subjectively perceived "imperfections", that are a result of a conflict or misfit of institutions merely represents the replacement of one less efficient transaction mode by another more efficient one. I.e. one set of institutional prescriptions for behavior is substituted by another set, the only merit of which is the actors' subjective perception of their improved correspondence with their objectives which, in turn, are derived from their unique institutional environments. Therefore, the attainment of party-efficiency for all actors involved in the transaction also implies allocative efficiency for the resulting transaction.

The determination of an efficiency gain then depends on whether, and if assessable, to what extent, realization of subjective objectives is improved. The main criterion used for such determination will be the reduction of transaction costs. The ensuing derivation of transaction cost-based efficiency criteria is therefore guided by this recognition of the relevance of the institutional determinants of objectives and subsequent behavior of the principal actors involved in international credit relationships.

Because the individual institutional environments of contracting parties differ the parties' subjectively established efficiency criteria may differ and even conflict with

---

16 It cannot be stressed often enough to think twice about the prejudicious quality of connotations of terminology derived from mathematical economic theory. Neither "imperfections" nor "efficiency" are per se desirable or undesirable. Only subjective opinion can assign value judgements to these concepts.

each other. Such a conflict of efficiency criteria can be derived from a conflict of objectives. What therefore may represent transaction costs for one party may not represent transaction costs for another party. When, finally, the institutional determinants of objectives and constraints are taken into account it becomes clear that all behavioral rules are derived from more fundamental behavioral rules. Thus, a perceived conflict of efficiency criteria may be caused by a conflict of institutions more fundamental than the objectives from which these criteria are derived. Figure 2 is an attempt to provide a broad-brush illustration of this hierarchical character of the evolution of institutions.

Figure 2: A Stylized Hierarchy of Social Institutions and Objectives

PRIMARY INSTITUTIONS:	- **Basic ethical standards** (protection of life) - **Basic cultural norms and values** (concepts of time and space, anthropocentrism, organismic individuality, religious beliefs, concepts of guilt, sense, god etc.)
SECONDARY INSTITUTIONS:	- **Societal values** (human rights, standards of welfare and social relations) - **Political objectives** (political stability, democracy, ideological adherence etc.) - **Economic and social objectives** (economic growth, justice)
TERTIARY INSTITUTIONS:	- **Specific laws and regulations** (criminal law, tax law, traffic law etc.) - **Business objectives** (profit maximization)

The relationship between institutions of one hierarchical level to institutions of the ensuing level can be characterized by the questions "what ought to be?" at one level - this is why we can speak at one time of objectives - and "how is this to be realized?" at the following level. The latter question shows why we can speak at the same time of institutions in the sense of rules. Although conflicts between fundamental ethical and economic, or "market-based" motives have always been noticed by economists (cf. *Arrow* [1974, 21]), topical examples for the high degree of such conflicts of objectives of all hierarchical dimensions of social institutions can be found in many less-industrialized countries[17].

Such examples are extreme poverty of a large part of the population in light of extreme wealth of a small part of the population, violation of human rights, the financing of military expenditures. Here, certain economic objectives may conflict with other more fundamental institutions in the respective cultural environments and thereby fail to serve their function for guiding behavior. However, often banks have lent to countries where conditions like these existed. The intricate relation between ethical, political and private business postulates in such instances is proof for the political clout commercial banks have when deciding on a loan to a particular country. It is an unanswered question so far whether banks should have this clout. This can also not be answered within this study.

For the ensuing analysis, however, emphasis will be given to efficiency criteria from the subjective perspective of private commercial banks. Such firm-specific economic efficiency criteria, however, can conflict with institutionalized decision criteria of an ethical or political nature as pointed out above. Criteria for efficiency need to be derived from institutionalized objectives because only these are stable and verifiable. Also, to formulate propositions for the explanation of empirical phenomena the institutional determinants of these phenomena have to be taken into account to the extent feasible.

Statements about the efficiency of an institutional change can only be made for an isolated problem context. This implies the existence of externalities, namely advantages or disadvantages for parties outside of the observed problem context. Such spill-overs can lead to costs to be borne by outside parties, that is, inefficiencies within an extended problem context. A truly holistic examination of economic phenomena can never yield statements about overall efficiency gains as only measurable aspects can be assessed in such a way.

Hence, it is not intended here to derive measures of efficiency from the idea that deviations from an ideal (perfect) world ex definitione create inefficiencies. A

---

17 The stylized three-level categorization used in figure 2 is for illustrative purposes only. It is certainly impossible to actually determine a number or thresholds of levels of institutions and their interdependence.

positive approach for determining efficiency gains for international credit relationships will start with an analysis of the institutional framework. For the assessment whether one financial product is more efficient than another one it is necessary to work with the premise that two specific stationary situations are comparable, which is based on the axioms of linearity and segmentability of time. This comparison should yield propositions about the advantages of particular transaction modes perceived by the parties considered in the problem context. This implies an identification of the changes in the institutional setting that have led to a change in this perception of advantages (cf. *Damm/Friedla/Schmidt* [1987, 147]). Therefore an analysis of the efficiency of innovative financial products requires an analysis of the institutional determinants of particular financial products, i.e. an institutional analysis.

An ideal world may only serve as a direction as long as the actors in question subscribe to such idealization. The better the institutional setting is known, the better is the explanation of observed behavior and of institutional influence on behavior, and the more accurate is the assessment of efficiency improvements. Thus, the point of departure is a given institutionally obfuscated creditor-lender relationship. An analysis of this institutional environment shall allow to identify institutions that pose obstacles for the use of more efficient transaction modes and would therefore lend themselves for more efficient design. The analysis can only account for an observable selection of institutions of significance.

An important methodological problem then is the measurement of efficiency gains. Often, a situation that is perceived as more efficient than another one does not necessarily result in a quantifiable benefit or cost reduction. Rather it could facilitate further improvements which then may be quantifiable. Or it may just reduce complexity for those involved in a transaction. For this reason, in the following, it will be attempted to derive criteria from the parties' objectives that serve to determine what constitutes costs or benefits of particular transaction modes. These criteria can also be used for the evaluation of some significant non-monetary or intangible effects that impact the risk/return relationship of the parties involved. With careful consideration of relevant aspects this analysis is of a qualitative, non-formal nature and may therefore itself display an unavoidable degree of "institutional obfuscation".

Given a verifiable firm-specific objective, e.g. to earn a certain profit from a transaction, efficiency gains in the realization of this objective can be achieved by reducing any perceived cost anticipated in this realization process. This requires the identification of what costs and revenues arise for what reasons. In this study, however, revenues will be regarded as fixed at the starting time of the contractual relationship. I.e. it will be assumed that loan contracts will not yield higher revenues than expected at the time of entry into the contractual relationship. Hence, reduction of expected revenues will be regarded as a cost. In this case, cost reduction represents a benefit and, thus, serves as a criterion for determining an efficiency gain. The main objective of banks involved in rescheduling country lending is assumed to be damage reduction by minimizing such expected costs, i.e. losses.

2.2. TRANSACTION COSTS

Before the transaction cost concept proposed in this study for an application to international credit relationships is presented the next two sections provide an introductory synopsis of some general aspects concerning the origin of the transaction cost approach and some methodological implications.

2.2.1. Origin of the Transaction Cost Approach

The concept of transaction costs has its roots in the seminal paper by *Coase* [1937]. It has further been developed by *Williamson* [1979, 1985] as a tool for explaining the organizational variety of economic transactions under an economic efficiency perspective[18]. "*Transaction costs are the economic equivalent of friction in physical systems*". (*Williamson* [1985, 19]) Transaction costs comprise all costs that arise as a consequence of the ex ante preparation and the ex post mastering efforts connected with a contractual relationship. These efforts are necessary because it is impossible to write contracts that perfectly account for all possible contingencies.

---

18 *Solo* [1967, 40passim] has developed a very similar concept for comparing different forms of economic organization and social systems. He has coined the term "institutional costs".

More generally, they arise with human interaction directed at reducing the uncertainty induced by the heterogeneity of the particular institutional (and natural) environments of individual actors by contracting. Such institutional conditions can either be deliberately imposed by political action or may emerge as a result of cultural - which implies economic - evolution from previous conditions. For example, at the time of the decision on the extension of a loan - i.e. ex ante - the lender faces uncertainty about the quality (cost categories) and quantity (amounts of costs and revenues) of the ex post consequences of a loan commitment. This is because except of the agreed-upon behavioral specifications of the loan contract the borrower's actions are based on a different set of behavioral rules than those of the lender.

The more pronounced the divergence of institutional conditions for the behavior of potential transacting parties is, the higher the costs of transacting will tend to be. In other words, the risk that unexpected behavior of other parties, which reduces expected benefits, will occur is the higher the greater the difference of institutional conditions relevant for the parties' actions. Apart from the behavioral rules specified for a particular transaction by means of a contract other behavioral rules also impact the contractual relationship. As long as these latter institutions are not familiar to all parties involved in the transaction the effect of the institutions specified is obfuscated by the institutions not specified as a result of the mutual dependance of institutions in guiding behavior.

If the institutional environments of transacting parties are highly homogeneous - e.g. among family members or among members of a firm with a distinctive "corporate culture" -, trust in counterparts can more easily be established. Harmonization of interests of transaction participants is more easily achieved (cf. *Williamson* [1979, 239]). Entering into transactions is thereby facilitated (cf. *Michaelis* [1985, 126seqq.]). Hence, the guiding maxim is: "*align transactions (which differ in their attributes) with governance structures (the costs and competencies of which differ) in a discriminating (mainly, transaction-cost economizing) way.*" (*Williamson* [1988, 571]) Governance structures here stand for the relevant institutional and contractual organizations or subcultures within which a transaction can be entered into, e.g. the complex of the rules of a market and its legal and non-legal ramifications, or rules of behavior within a firm - i.e. its corporate culture.

Besides self-interest seeking by transaction participants another important assumption that underlies the ensuing analysis is bounded rationality. On the basis of the information at hand the actors are consciously aware of their choices and decide in pursuit of subjectively perceived advantages. However, they also know that more information would yield better choices but confine themselves to decisions under bounded rationality because they perceive a limit for the additional cost they can bear to obtain more information.

Generally, sources for the emergence of transaction costs can be identified as follows (cf. *Breeden/Toumanoff* [1985, 164seqq.]):

(1) Social and cultural barriers, such as different values, prejudices, fear, languages, religions, traditions, and customs;

(2) technical, geographical, and time-related barriers to exchange;

(3) governments as responsible creators of laws, regulations, and price controls.

Hence, when all social interaction is viewed as an exchange process, every institution (e.g. laws, manners, as well as the concepts of the firm and the market) can be interpreted as serving to reduce the perceived transaction costs of social interaction. In fact, the transaction cost approach introduces the principle of evolution into economic analysis as all evolutionary "progress" can be interpreted as an infinite process of transaction cost economizing. Criteria for efficiency evaluations like for example the Pareto criterion can then be viewed as intersubjectively agreed-upon standards of measurement for the improvement of the survival potential of institutions in the evolutionary process.

2.2.2. Methodological Implications

The transaction cost approach to economic analysis is interrelated with the property rights theory[19] and is based on the goal-oriented paradigm of maximizing subjectively perceived benefits by choosing among alternative patterns of institutional and contractual organization, also termed governance structures. Given a particular institutionalized organization for economic transactions, it is

---

19 V. *Alchian/Demsetz* [1972] and [1973], *Demsetz* [1964], *Furubotn/Pejovich* [1974], and *Gäfgen* [1984].

presumed that an actor will switch to an alternative organization if the expected switching costs and differential costs relative to the alternative are lower than the expected additional benefits.

Positive or negative externalities may arise for "non"-associated actors because the actor does not perceive any pay-off from the "internalization" of such costs and/or benefits of third parties. Similarly, external costs perceived to arise to third parties do not induce them to intervene into the causal transaction as long as the transaction costs of such intervention are higher than the perceived expected negative externalities[20].

A weighty implication of the assumptions of the transaction cost approach is that it does not provide an explanation why a particular new transaction mode emerged, but only why a conceivable transaction mode can be judged to be preferable to another conceivable transaction mode (cf. *Kieser* [1988, 316]). It is only possible to explain why a new transaction mode is used after it has been "invented", i.e. why it is institutionalized. It does not explain what the particular problems of the inefficient transaction mode are as long as no superior transaction mode is conceived. It only explains which transaction mode is more efficient once it is already conceived. Hence, transaction costs provide no tool for an explanation of the emergence of innovations or, for that matter, institutions, but only for an ex post explanation of why a new transaction mode can be termed innovation.

Two other problems of the concept are central for the validity of its application to economic analysis and management issues in particular. One is the difficulty to distinguish transaction costs from production costs, operating costs, transportation costs, overhead costs, or other categories of costs that are readily quantifiable for management accounting purposes (cf. *Michaelis* [1985, 89]). These definitions are based upon firm-specific concerns such as the type or function of inputs or the location within a firm's organizational system whereas transaction costs are based upon transaction-specific concerns. However, this merely represents a terminological problem which can be overcome by further nominal definition of transaction cost categories for specific contexts.

---

20 For an evaluation and critique of the limits of the neoclassical marginal utility program, which lies at the foundation of the transaction cost approach cf. *Ulrich* [1986, 251passim].

The other problem consists of the universal applicability of a term "cost" which does not need to be quantifiable. This can lead to a tautology in the description of relevant economic problems - all at once every interaction becomes a transaction and every perceived negative influence can be interpreted as a cost. Also for most economic activities, and in particular in international lending by banks, it will often be difficult or impossible to measure transaction costs as no transaction-specific measurement technique exists. Most of these costs are contained in salaries, overhead, the cost of equipment, taxes, cost of capital, fees for services rendered by other firms, and losses from defaults. The establishment of transaction-specific measurement techniques may be too costly and may prevent the transaction in the first place.

The perception of costs is a purely subjective matter. One bank may perceive a certain cost that another may not. However, it is relatively less expensive for one bank to take into account costs that other banks perceive as well. In this case the costs of measuring such costs do not impair in principle an individual bank's competitive position vis-à-vis other banks. Should a bank perceive costs which other banks do not perceive it may put itself in a competitive disadvantage as long as other banks will not later on perceive the same costs. Despite of this, many transactions are entered into without the possibility to measure the costly effects of one party's behavior on the other party. It cannot therefore be denied that such immeasurable transaction costs are a relevant economic phenomenon.

On the other hand, this is considered to be the major drawback of the concept of transaction costs which has so far offered only limited transferability to the use as a criterion for "numbers-based" decisions in practice[21] - it is still basically a speculative theory relying on its heuristic potential only (cf. *Budäus* [1988, 47]). However, from a methodological perspective this caveat is simply the result of a scientistic desire to establish "objective" consistency. Quantifiable measurement criteria are themselves based upon theories which enjoy very far-reaching acceptance. In any case, context-specific definition of transaction costs is therefore required.

---

21 For an example of such an application v. *Jung/Spreemann* [1989].

Finally, such definition is also necessary as the application of transaction cost arguments for the explanation of perceived efficiency improvements through institutional innovations will otherwise ultimately lead to an infinite regress. This is because the identification of particular transaction costs - and, thus, criteria for efficiency improvements - depend upon some mentally conceived stationary pretransactional institutional set-up. These criteria and the institutional set-up on which they rely, however, are already the result of previous transaction cost economizing. Hence, the definition of transaction costs at one "point in time" depends upon the definition of transaction costs at a previous "point in time", which again depends upon the definition of transaction costs at a previous "point in time" and so on. For methodological reasons, this infinite regress has to be artificially interrupted in order to save the very notion of party-efficiency.

2.2.3. A Taxonomy of Transaction Costs

Williamson [1979, 245], who focuses on physical product transactions, distinguishes between production costs and transaction costs. In finance the object of a transaction is a financial service. The product transferred under a loan contract is not of a physical nature. It consists of the temporary use of money, i.e. the temporary use of a standardized medium of the communication of subjective valuations.

As "*a consensus on transaction costs is lacking*" (*Williamson* [1979, 234]) anyway, in the following a taxonomy is proposed which is intended to reflect particular properties of financial transactions. Here, *Williamson's* approach only has an inspirational function. It is important to note that in order to compare different contracting modes for financial transactions, the focus of analysis has to be on the transaction itself (cf. *Commons* [1990/1934, 58]). Then, transaction costs are the costs that are perceived as a consequence of engaging in a transaction[22]. Therefore, all costs that arise with the set-up and execution of a contract, and,

---

22 It is important to note that "costs" in this usage also stand for disadvantages as they are perceived. This is in line with *Coase's* [1937, 391] interpretation. Monetary quantification is not required. Cf. also *Michaelis* [1985, 78seqq.].

thus, the associated transaction, play a role in assessing the relative advantages of one transaction mode versus another transaction mode[23].

For the purposes of this study the following taxonomy is proposed[24]:

(1) **Set-up costs** comprise the costs of drafting and negotiating a contract.

(2) **Information costs** include the costs of searching for, obtaining, assimilating, and interpreting information on the appropriateness of the counterparties to the contract and environmental factors. These environmental factors comprise selected institutional determinants for the expected subsequent behavior of the parties to the contract. Also monitoring and state verification costs are subsumed under this category.

(3) **Participation costs** include the costs of assuming and executing the rights and duties implied in the contract through the respective governance structure.

(4) **Modification costs** include the costs that result from maladaption of the contract, the costs of successive adaption of the contract to unfolding events, and haggling costs involved in adjusting contractual positions.

Furthermore, an additional categorization is proposed which extends this taxonomy to include the dimension of time. As to the time of the emergence of transaction costs, ex ante costs (**preparation costs**) and ex post costs (**enforcement**

---

23 It appears at least conceivable to link the proposed transaction cost taxonomy with the contribution margin concept in production theory. However, as some elements of the cost categories used in the following are not readily quantifiable, this question will not be investigated further.

24 The separation of transaction cost categories as established here does not exactly correspond to the one *Williamson* [1985] introduced. It also draws on *Franke/Hax* [1988, 334passim] who apply transaction cost arguments to financial claims analysis. *Jensen/Meckling* [1976] established the notion of "agency costs" that include bonding costs, monitoring costs (which correspond to post-contractual information costs) and a "residual loss". Agency costs are conceived as arising as a consequence of reducing the conflict potential inherent in principal-agent relationships. A critique of the concept of agency costs is offered by *Schneider* [1987, 553seqq.].

costs[25]) can be distinguished. Preparation costs comprise the costs necessary to enter into a contract. By this definition they only include set-up costs and information costs. Enforcement costs are those arising from executing the contractually specified performance and all other measures taken to ensure the enforcement of the contract. They include information, participation, and modification costs. Figure 3 illustrates the linkage between these definitions.

Figure 3: Transaction Cost Categories

		Type			
		Set-up Costs	**Information Costs**	**Participation Costs**	**Modification Costs**
Time	**Preparation costs** (ex ante)	X	X	n.a.	n.a.
	Enforcement costs (ex post)	n.a.	X	X	X

An important condition for the application of these transaction cost definitions is the definition of contract. For the purposes of this study a loan contract is represented by the originally committed funds as its asset base. The change of original contractual terms is not regarded as a separate new contract but rather as an amendment, i.e. a modification of contractual terms. Here, even the transformation of the quality of the committed funds as f.i. in the case of a conversion of debt into equity (debt equity swap) is not interpreted as a new contract. From a legal perspective, however, a new contract would be assumed to exist[26].

---

25 *Rowe* [1989, 91seq.] also introduces the term "enforcement cost" as an ingredient for a concept for assessing the efficiency of institutions. However, he does not subdivide this term into further cost categories.

26 However, even among legal scholars there is no clear-cut answer of when exactly it can be assumed that a new contract replaces an old one or whether one contract is merely amended without explicit termination (cf. *Horn* [1984, 720seq.]). For a description of this process of contractual change v. *Messer* [1989, 35seqq.].

Examples for components of transaction costs in international lending can be outlined as follows. Set-up costs may consist of lawyers' fees, salaries of loan officers, traders and negotiators, and the associated overhead and equipment costs. Information costs arise when information is perceived to be scarce or insufficient relative to some standard. If information costs are perceived as high, transactions tend to be of a short-term character or may not take place at all (cf. *Guttentag/Herring* [1986a, 78]). They are reflected in, e.g., the costs of staff for screening country risks, costs of associated equipment and overhead, fees for information services provided by other firms etc.

Participation costs include all costs that have to be incurred to effect the contractually specified performance and all costs that arise as a consequence of these actions. Besides loan management costs, e.g. costs of personnel, overhead, and equipment involved in the necessary disbursement and collection of funds, communication, and maintenance of relations to regulators and the public, they also include the costs of obtaining the necessary assets required to fulfill contractual obligations and taxes to be paid as a consequence of the transaction.

Modification costs comprise all costs that result from changing the contractual rights and obligations in order to maintain the contractual relationship, i.e. in order to avoid an impairment of the asset base of the contract. These are f.i. the costs incurred in reaching rescheduling agreements and the costs of engaging in debt swaps. Again these costs are mainly reflected in salaries, overhead and equipment costs, fees for services rendered by lawyers and investment banks.

To be able to bear transaction costs, banks charge interest and fees. In lending, interest rate spreads usually include also a risk premium. Contracts give rise to the emergence of these costs and their allocation among contracting parties. Transaction costs tend to be higher the higher the default risk as contractual specifications will become more complex. Depending upon the nature of the contractual relationship, its time frame, its object, environmental conditions, and the frequency of occurence of comparable relationships certain types of transaction costs may dominate over others.

As will be shown, in international credit relationships enforcement costs in the forms of information and modification costs are of relatively greater importance for lenders. Within a domestic context government agencies assume a large portion of the costs of contract enforcement and monitoring. In an international context, however, because of the lack of an effective enforcement system, most of these costs have to be borne by contracting parties. Additional information costs arise because of the lack of international supervisory regulations and the factually exclusive discretion of sovereign debtors to report relevant information.

2.3. CAUSES FOR THE EMERGENCE OF TRANSACTION COSTS IN INTERNATIONAL DEBT MANAGEMENT

International economic transactions are prone to high degrees of institutional obfuscation because of the heterogeneity of institutional conditions in various countries. In a "domestic" environment transaction costs are perceived to be relatively lower as the outcome of transactions and effects of institutional change are more predictable. Here, institutional conditions are perceived to be more coherent and less diverse. In the international context such coherence is far less pronounced. Cultural and in particular jurisdictional diversity as well as the consequential non-existence of credible international legal recourses lead to higher transaction cost barriers for transactions.

2.3.1. Obstacles for the Enforcement of International Loan Contracts

Measures to reduce transaction costs depend on the degree of enforceability or party-enforceability[27] of a contract. Party-enforceability again depends on the parties' relative bargaining power concerning a particular claim (cf. *Lessard* [1989, 204]). Enforceability of contractual claims against a sovereign borrower through the legal process in cases of default is obstructed primarily as a consequence of the sovereign's immunity against legal action by a foreign authority. Hence, many international lending contracts contain a sovereign immunity waiver which is intended to reduce enforcement costs by allowing to sue a sovereign entity. However, redress in any chosen court may not be effective, because it is generally impossible or too costly to expropriate assets - even if only to prevent escalation

27 The term "party-enforceability" is preferred to the anthropomorphic term "self-enforceability" which is customary in finance theory although it is obvious that a contract cannot enforce itself and because it carries with it the connotation that it is only the behavioral rules contained in the contract which determine its enforceability.

(cf. *Kaletsky* [1985, 22seqq.]). Legal redress would also be questionable in case of proceedings in a court of the debtor country.

In addition, the attachment or sequestration of assets of non-governmental origin is obstructed by the "veil of incorporation" doctrine which excludes individual, i.e. including corporate, citizens from the liability of their government (*ibid.* [27seq.]). Also the indirect costs banks would have to face in case of effecting legal sanctions after a de jure default have so far contributed to the lack of enforceability of loan contracts[28].

Similarly, provisions which require the borrower to use the debt only for specific undertakings or to implement certain policies thought to be conducive to effect eventual repayment are not directly enforceable vis-à-vis the lender. To circumvent this problem often the attempt was made to engage an international organization like the IMF or the World Bank in a debt rescheduling in order to better control the build-up of debt and debt service capacity (conditionality). However, such interference did not always yield the desired results.

The fact that international loan contracts are honored after all - at least to a certain extent - requires the existence of an enforcement mechanism independent of the explicit contractual content. It has been pointed out by various authors (cf. *Dale* [1984, 80] and *Kaletsky* [1985]) that a complex of implicit threats and promises by the contracting parties - and, thus, the costs thereof - accounts for the maintenance of credit relationships. In other words, international loan contracts display a certain degree of party-enforceability.

The most obvious threat, resp. promise, at the disposal of lending banks consists of the possibility to stop, resp. continue, financial relationships with the borrower[29]. Such actions, however, imply transaction costs and may not be viable as long as f.i. cooperative solutions are perceived to be less costly. The borrower, however, has

---

28 These costs comprise the losses from default which in some cases may threaten the survival of a bank and costs arising from systemic effects on international financial relationships (cf. *Kaletsky* [1985, 29seqq.]).

29 It is necessary to distinguish between various kinds of financial transactions (short-term, long-term, trade credit, equity investments, etc.) and to analyze the potentially different interests of different lenders and investors in order to assess the validity of such a sanction (cf. *Kaletsky* [1985, 33seqq.]).

the same option. The clout of its threat, resp. promise, depends on the size of the debt relative to the banks' ability to absorb loan losses, expectations of lenders about the attractiveness of future transactions, and foreign policy considerations of the respective governments, i.e. the likelihood of a bail-out of banks by their domicile country governments.

Closely connected with the issue of unenforceability is the non-existence of institutionalized sources for redress. In the context of domestic corporate finance such redress can be derived from the existence of the concept of financial liability which is embodied in institutions like equity capital, collateral, or letters of awareness, and the existence of some form of corporate bankruptcy code (cf. *Deppe* [1987]). In a domestic context, losses from credit transactions therefore usually are of a definite amount at some specific date. Losses resulting from international credit relationships, however, may never be quantifiable - except in cases of outright repudiation (cf. *Dale* [1984, 80]).

2.3.2. Examples of Enforcement Cost Inducing Behavior

For this study, enforcement costs are recognized as more important than preparation costs. The underlying loan contracts, as defined above, have already been entered into. Innovative transaction modes, then, are interpreted as solutions of attempts to minimize the transaction costs associated with the enforcement of the original contractual repayment obligations of the borrowers.

In order to understand the difference in adaptability of one transaction mode versus another transaction mode within a particular institutional framework or governance structure, the causes of cost differences have to be identified. In other words, it is necessary to determine ex post by what means one transaction mode allows a more efficient solution to enforcement problems than another one. Therefore, in the following, selected enforcement cost inducing behavioral phenomena relevant for credit relationships between private banks and rescheduling countries will be identified. All of these are of a post-contractual nature and contribute to behavioral uncertainty in general.

From the perspective of a creditor bank any action that reduces the probability to enforce an existing loan contract involves a cost for the creditor. This is because, ex post, it reduces the expected net present value of the associated financial claim. It does not matter whether such action is taken by the debtor, other creditor banks, or other actors like law makers in banks' domicile countries. This happens in the context of international lending because of the general impossibility to write complete contracts and the lack of an effective enforcement mechanism in case such actions indirectly lead to the violation of contractual stipulations. Parties can have strategic reasons to conceal their preferences (cf. *Buchanan* [1984, 12]). This may lead to misunderstandings and future conflicts between contracting parties.

For instance, the fact that most international loans to sovereign debtors did not contain specifications as to the use of borrowed funds has raised enforcement costs substantially. This is because the debtor in this case is not required to channel borrowed funds into productive export-oriented investments that ensure future debt service ability but rather may spend them for consumptive purposes. Although rescheduling countries have followed different policies, extensive use of funds for consumer imports has been observed in several of the highly indebted countries (cf. *Sachs* [1989a, 14]). Other examples of enforcement cost inducing debtor behavior from creditor banks' perspective are capital flight and corruption. However, not only debtor behavior but also creditor behavior may increase enforcement costs. Namely free rider and herding phenomena are examples.

2.3.2.1. Capital Flight

"*Capital flight can be defined as the reported and unreported acquisition of foreign assets by the non-bank sector and some elements of the public sector*" (*Morgan Guaranty* [1986, 13]) The explanation of capital flight rests on a similarly complex multitude of determinants as country risk[30]. In fact, capital flight constitutes a codeterminant of country risk and raises enforcement costs. In essence, perceived differences of risk-adjusted returns in source and haven countries are the quantifiable base for decisions on exporting capital. No exact figures exist on the amount of flight capital that has left rescheduling countries. Many attempts to estimate the size of capital flight have been made in the recent past (*Cuddington* [1986], *Morgan Guaranty* [1986])[31].

---

30 V. section 2.4.1.

31 A BIS study estimated that some US$ 55 billion left Latin America (except Venezuela) from 1978 to 1982 (*Ayittey* [1986]).

Williamson and Lessard [1987, 56] distinguish two general theories to explain capital flight. However, both focus exclusively on debtor country factors as causes for capital flight. One identifies fears of currency devaluation, inflation, fiscal deficits, low growth, and debt overhang as constituents of an adverse investment climate which induces capital flight. The other theory stresses discriminatory treatment of resident capital as an incentive and points to causes such as the imposition of certain tax policies, financial repression, nonavailability of foreign-exchange denomination of claims, and subordination to nonresident claims in crisis events. In addition, factors like expectations about political stability, likelihood of expropriations, opposition to actual political forces can be cited as causes for capital flight.

However, as only the perceived differences in the institutional structure of source and haven countries motivate capital flows, all possible causes identified in a source country may as well be identified in inverted form in haven countries as incentives for capital flight. Thus a reduction of capital flight could theoretically also be achieved by adjusting haven country institutions. Whether such a change is preferable to an adjustment of source country institutions is ultimately a question of subjective political opinion and lies therefore outside the scope of economic analysis. For instance, a significant determinant for capital flight from Latin American countries is the heterogeneity of tax laws of source and destination countries. For the case of the USA *McLure* [1988] has shown that US-American tax laws in particular present an inducement for many Latin American citizens to engage in such tax law arbitrage and to transfer capital to the USA.

2.3.2.2. Corruption

Costs can also arise as a consequence of differing moral convictions. The most visible such phenomenon is corruption. In many less-industrialized countries the ability to realize desired projects financed through international loans and a project's or certain policy's effectiveness often depends on the satisfaction of personal material interests (cf. *FAZ* [21. März 1988]). Thus, corruption has been identified as a factor that led to the diversion of borrowed funds into undesired uses from the perspective of lenders, thereby raising the costs of enforcement of claims (cf. *Mendelowitz* [1989, 1]). The honesty of public officers is a precondition for the establishment of policies conducive to serve the banks' interests (cf. *Hakim*

[1985, 24] and *Salom* [1985, 126seq.]). Furthermore, corruption may fuel capital flight as illicit incomes of debtor country residents are probably better concealed in foreign bank accounts (cf. *Williamson/Lessard* [1987, 34]).

2.3.2.3. Free Rider Behavior

When fresh money commitments form part of reschedulings, banks with relatively large exposures depend on the participation of the greater number of banks with smaller exposures. A failure to keep a debtor country on its repayment plan and to prevent further reschedulings or default will impose higher costs on larger banks. Smaller banks, on the other hand, benefit from the strengthening effect of new lending by larger banks on their claims (cf. *Cline* [1987, 8seq.]). These may therefore have an incentive to free ride by not going along with fresh money lending (cf. *Buchanan* [1984, 12]). Thus, additional participation costs may arise to banks with large exposures. To avoid this phenomenon, equal treatment of each creditor has been made a fundamental principle of syndicated loans to rescheduling countries. Several clauses, contained in practically all credit contracts with sovereign borrowers, provide for this equality of treatment[32].

Free riding may also be perceived by banks that do not take part in debt swap schemes as, for instance, through exit bonds[33]. The sharing clause[34] which provides for equal treatment of all creditors as to receiving payments from the debtor may therefore present a threat for banks that choose to participate in such schemes (cf. *Williamson, J.* [1988, 23]). Here, the argument is similar. Other banks may go to court in case of a violation of the clause because they would otherwise have to bear additional participation costs as a consequence of perceived free riding of exiting banks.

Reasons for this free riding by some banks, i.e. particularly smaller and some European banks, are differing strategies and sizes of exposure. This leads to different transaction cost perceptions and thereby creates incentives to free riding

---

32 V. section 3.2.3.

33 V. section 3.3.2.2.

34 V. section 3.2.3.4.

from the perspective of other banks[35]. These incentives will be perceived particularly by smaller banks that view their retreat from credit relationships with a rescheduling country as insignificant for improving the financial condition of a debtor country. The accumulation of such perceptions among a large group of banks, however, may lead to the infeasibility of implementing a specific debt relief scheme or participation in fresh money exercises and thereby raise modification costs.

At the initial stage of the formation of a syndicated credit agreement, smaller banks have usually relied on the credit and country analysis already performed by the larger leading banks[36]. Thus, smaller banks behaved as free riders as they did not have to incur the information costs of the leading banks. Here, some banks incur information costs which others do not.

2.3.2.4. Herding

It has often been suggested that commercial banks displayed a group behavior that can be termed "herding", "pack instinct", "clubbing", or "follow the leader" (cf. *Lessard* [1983, 530] and *Sidler* [1983, 142]) which may have been furthered by the widespread application of the syndication mechanism. This transaction mode is perceived as reducing the enforcement costs for claims as all creditors act as a large group supporting each other. It also is perceived as reducing the risk of regulatory change as supervisors cannot as easily differentiate between banks with different exposures and business focuses.

Also the reliance by followers on the country analysis performed by the leaders indicates the inclination of followers to club, thus to benefit from information costs already incurred by the lead banks. As the initial decisions and impetus to lend to a sovereign borrower is thought to have originated with the "leaders of the pack"

---

35 Cf. f.i. the analysis in section 5.3.1.

36 "*This meant that many small- and medium-sized banks, with little or no previous experience in sovereign lending, became active in the market.*

The new participants relied almost exclusively on the money-center banks, which were responsible for arranging the syndicated credits. The primary source of information for these new participants was the information or "placement" memorandum in which a country's economic and political situation was described." (*Bogdanowicz-Bindert/Sacks* [1984, 71]) the followers in this sense can be interpreted as free riders. In a statistical test of the portfolio allocation decisions of large and small US-American banks *Jain/Gupta* [1987], however, found only very weak evidence, if any, of herding behavior.

On the other hand, herding contributes to increasing the risk that risky behavior of one bank by being imitated by others can lead to substantial frictions in the whole financial system. This, in response, may require regulatory action which may further restrain bank behavior (cf. *Franke* [1987a, 438]).

2.4. TRANSACTION RISKS

In any economic transaction there is the possibility that the actual outcome of the transaction does not coincide with the expected outcome. This possibility is termed "risk". A negative deviation from a given expected outcome is a "downside" risk, a positive deviation is an "upside" risk. The attainment of a specified profit objective requires that all risks implied in the entirety of a bank's business transactions are contained within certain limits. Although a bank manager would not extend a particular loan when the service of this loan is in doubt, the existing portfolio of loans always contains a risky portion as information about the future is uncertain.

The expected net present value (ENPV) of a series of disbursements and repayments of principal and interest is the most common measure for assessing the benefits associated with a particular financial claim. The discount factor used in this calculation implies an evaluation of the potential impact of the riskiness of this loan. Innovations that reduce the expected impact of a particular risk reduce the probability of costs arising from future events associated with such risks. This can generally be expressed in terms of ENPV and thus be made operational to assess the efficiency of an innovation.

Most measures taken to manage risks are costly. Such risk management costs can be viewed as the costs of preparing to engage in risky transactions. Under this perspective, transaction costs would also comprise risk management costs because the enforceability of contracts is increased with the reduction of transaction risks. Those banks that have comparative advantage in bearing risks therefore also face comparatively lower transaction costs than other banks in this respect. Risk management costs may be of a general or transaction-specific nature. Also the cost of the actual assumption of risks as reflected in risk premiums - which is usually not regarded as a transaction cost - can either be general or transaction-specific. Reduction of risk and risk management costs can thus serve as another criterion for the identification of efficiency improvements.

The perception of transaction risks is reflected in expected enforcement costs. A reduction of risks hence may imply an eventual reduction of enforcement costs. The reduction of transaction risks is introduced here as a separate criterion because it points to further important sources of enforcement problems that can be expressed in familiar financial terminology. However, for the analysis presented in this study, risk reduction will in most cases implicitly be treated within the context of applying the criterion of enforcement cost reduction.

2.4.1. A Taxonomy of Transaction Risks

The following risks are relevant for banks' international lending to less-industrialized countries:

(1) The **risk of regulatory change** originates with the governments of banks' domicile countries and describes the potentially adverse effects of a change of tax, supervisory, and other laws.

(2) **Interest rate risk** originates from the actions of all market participants. From the perspective of an individual bank it mainly becomes relevant because of maturity transformation between asset and liability items.

(3) **Exchange rate risk** also originates from the actions of all market participants. It describes the possibility that the value of one currency in terms of another currency may decrease.

(4) **Country risk** is the dominant risk category in international lending relationships with sovereign borrowers and will therefore here be treated in more detail. It is a subcategory of the risk of non-payment. The risk of non-payment originates with the borrower and concerns the possibility of the temporary (liquidity risk) or final (solvency risk) cessation of due payments. In addition to the non-payment risk associated with an individual project or

> firm a transfer risk arises from a government's inability (transfer risk) or unwillingness (political or sovereign risk) to provide the required amounts of foreign exchange for debt service.

Attempts to conceptualize the phenomenon of country risk started with application of tools and terminology derived from domestic corporate finance. This is why, still today, authors try to analyze country risk by separating a debtor's illiquidity from his insolvency. "*Illiquidity means that a debtor cannot service the debt on the agreed time table, but in principle, can generate a present value of debt service equal to that contracted. Insolvency means that it is impossible to service the debts in full on any time table.*" (*Dornbusch* [1986, 89]) With this definition, insolvency can never arise as long as a country is able to restrict imports, expand exports, or reduce foreign exchange outflows sufficient to maintain solvency status (cf. *ibid.*).

There is, however, the possibility that the government is incompetent to implement policies to maintain solvency status or has reached a threshold above which it is no longer able to politically enforce such a status. The latter could be interpreted as to represent the result of this incompetence. Sovereign insolvency thus is ultimately a political concept, depending at least to a large part on the actions and inactions of political entities[37].

Of course, a government may be restricted in implementing certain policies not only by domestic political forces, but also by adverse developments of the international economy as well as by political pressures from abroad. But in any case, a measure of sovereign insolvency can only be determined taking into account the political abilities and forces at play. However, these can only be assessed qualitatively. Therefore it is impossible to derive an "objective", quantifiable measure for country risk. For instance, the application of some rating scheme and its subsequent consideration in a country risk adjusted discount rate may be perceived as enabling an approximation of a measure of country risk, however, these approaches finally result in self-deception if their subjective nature is overlooked.

---

37 Cf. also the discussion by *Dale* [1984, 78seq.]. Insofar as a government's decision to default is viewed as a rational one economists have offered a variety of models trying to explain country risk as the result of a verifiable cost-benefit analysis of the borrowing country. For a survey of this literature v. *Saunders* [1986] and also *Eaton/Gersovitz/Stiglitz* [1986].

Equally ambivalent is the attempt to operationalize country risk by differentiating a sovereign debtor's "unability" and "unwillingness" to pay. *Dale* [1984, 79] points out that many reschedulings may have been impelled by implicit threats of default but that it is impossible to determine any clear threshold at which one could speak of either unability or unwillingness to service debt. However, this distinction highlights the central reason why country risk is exclusively perceived as an international phenomenon. In a domestic context legal institutions provide for enforcement modes that prohibit unwillingness as a formal reason for non-payment of contractual claims. Although unwillingness may exist as a motive for the debtor, the possibility of legal redress either transforms this motive formally into unability to pay or enforces due payments through application of law.

Dale cites further differences between domestic credit risks and country risk [1984, 80seq.]: Actions of a government undertaken in order to restore liquidity for debt service cannot be compared with actions a domestic firm may undertake because of a conflict between objectives of a political nature (prevention of unemployment, provision of social services etc.) with objectives of a private firm which usually follows the same objectives as its shareholders. Another reason for the relevance of country risk as a separate risk category is the high amount of credit a sovereign borrower usually demands. This is one of the reasons that gave rise to the need for bank syndicates comprising several hundred separate banking organizations. This, in turn, provides an indirect link to phenomena like "free riding", and provides the borrower with options for different creditor treatment[38].

A so-called "agency" problem emerges with the role of the government as representative and moderator of the citizens of a debtor country The interests of the members of the government often diverge from the interests of the citizens. The situation is similar to the relationship between owners of a firm and its managers. Only in a democratic setting the period of office of government officials may be limited. Hence, country risk may not only arise because of a particular behavior of government officials as representatives of citizens' interests but also as a result of a conflict of interests between citizens and members of the government.

---

38 It is the function of the cross-default clause to prevent such discrimination of creditors. Cf. section 3.2.3.1.

2.4.2. Risk Management

Various methods can be applied to achieve an effective management of risks. Three categories of methods can be distinguished (*Franke/Hax* [1988, 230seq.]). Diversification of risks within a particular portfolio of assets consists of the selection of investments in new assets and the restructuring, i.e. the investment in and divestment of existing assets. Effective diversification minimizes the correlation of possible causes of loan losses and thereby reduces the average value of loan losses among all assets. Loans can be diversified by selecting borrowers, contractual patterns, amounts, currency denominations, and maturities.

A second class of methods consists of the prevention and limitation of damages arising from risky investments. Here, the emphasis is on the shielding and protection of the size and composition of a particular portfolio. Such measures may be unrelated to the investment in question and are costly. The most important measure is the establishment of an adequate equity cover through (stock) capital, earnings and reserves. This provision serves as an unspecific precaution to absorb actual loan losses. Part of a bank's business policy therefore has to be directed at protecting its equity position - the basic, legally stipulated condition for the operation of a bank. Also investments in technical equipment for the protection against damages from fraud, theft, or fire etc. belong into this category.

A third possible way of managing risks is the transfer or shifting, and the division of risks. These methods aim at diversifying risks among various portfolios. Risk transfers can be realized through market-based transactions where one party assumes a particular damage potential for a certain fee. The most common transaction mode of this kind is an insurance contract. But also hedging instruments like futures and option contracts serve this function. Division of risks allows to reduce the potential impact of the risk of a particular investment by partitioning the amount of the investment among a group of investors. Techniques like re-insurance in the insurance industry and syndication and project finance in banking fulfill this function.

2.5. SUMMARY

Besides providing some essential definitions, this chapter served to introduce two central concepts for the ensuing analysis of innovative transaction modes in international debt management. One is the notion of financial culture which is represented by the complex of all institutional prescriptions of behavior for financial transactions. On the basis of a three-dimensional classification of institutions the concept of financial culture serves to organize the various institutional influences on banks' behavior in rescheduling country debt management and, thus, also serves as a terminological structure for this study.

The second central concept is a transaction cost approach designed to reflect some particular properties of credit relationships between private commercial banks and sovereign governments. Here, reduction of transaction costs is proposed as the primary efficiency criterion to be applied in the course of the analysis. Following *Commons* and *Williamson* in their assertion that the transaction is the appropriate ultimate unit of analysis, transaction cost categories are defined on the basis of types of activities necessary to maintain the contractual relationships that underlie transactions (set-up, information, participation, and modification) and on the basis of the time they arise, i.e. before the contract is entered into (preparation) or afterwards (enforcement).

The proposition of this approach has also been motivated by the desire to apply a concept of efficiency to the subject of the study that allows to take account of the fact that cost perceptions depend on the unique institutional conditions for each individual party. Whereas the concept of allocative efficiency only provides a transsubjective criterion for the ex post validity of any transaction, party-efficiency provides a criterion that can serve to compare alternative transactions ex ante and ex post from a subjective, party-specific perspective.

This is why the concept of party-efficiency will be employed here as it is able to account for the institutional causes of party-specific cost perceptions. As will be shown, these causes can be found in the complex of institutional prescriptions for each party's behavior relevant for the transaction in question. As the proposed transaction cost criteria depend on the subjective institutional conditions of individual party. Whereas the concept of allocative efficiency only provides a transsubjective criterion for the ex post validity of any transaction, party-efficiency provides a criterion that can serve to compare alternative transactions ex ante and ex post from a subjective, party-specific perspective.

This is why the concept of party-efficiency will be employed here as it is able to account for the institutional causes of party-specific cost perceptions. As will be shown, these causes can be found in the complex of institutional prescriptions for each party's behavior relevant for the transaction in question. As the proposed transaction cost criteria depend on the subjective institutional conditions of contracting parties it is natural that these criteria can differ, or even conflict, among the parties.

Another efficiency criterion, which is introduced separately, is the reduction of transaction risks. The taxonomy of transaction risks put forward here defines - in familiar financial terminology - some potential causes for the emergence of enforcement costs. This is why the risks involved in engaging into transactions are reflected in expected enforcement costs. Therefore, reduction of transaction risks will specifically be referred to only in selected instances.

3. THE EVOLUTION OF INNOVATIONS IN INTERNATIONAL DEBT MANAGEMENT

This chapter provides a brief outline of the perceived causes and development of the debt crisis and describes the most relevant product-related institutional aspects of rescheduling country lending. Finally, those innovations are presented which will be the subject of further analysis in chapter 5.

3.1. THE INTERNATIONAL DEBT CRISIS

3.1.1. Economic Background

International lending can be divided into long-term (3 - 10 years), medium-term (1 - 3 years), and short-term (up to one year) lending. The category short-term consists mainly of trade finance transaction modes. Two categories of external debt can be distinguished: Official debt consists of government-backed loans (credit relationships between governments and credit relationships between debtor countries and international organizations like the IMF and development banks) and private debt.

Traditionally, the two basic transaction modes for sovereign states to borrow external funds on a medium- or long-term basis from private sources are international bonds or similar securities and loans from foreign commercial banks. Until 1973, and especially before 1931, international bonds had been the dominating mechanism for these countries to obtain external funds (cf. *Folkerts-Landau* [1985, 320seq.]). The following table shows the respective volumes of both transaction modes for the years 1970-1985. Although bank lending is dominant throughout bond financing has increased and new bank lending has dropped sharply since 1981.

The source of the unprecedented expansion of commercial bank lending to less-industrialized countries have been OPEC surplus funds channeled into the Euromarket after the first sharp rise in oil prices in 1973. External indebtedness of Latin American countries, for instance, increased by 25% p.a. on average from 1973 to 1976 (*Röller* [1987, 7]). Institutional reasons such as the lack of reserve requirements in the Euromarket and the availability of the then innovative transaction mode of syndicated roll-over lending contributed to the rapid surge in international lending.

Table 2: Foreign Borrowing by Less-Industrialized Countries from Private Creditors 1970-1985 (US$ million)[a]

Year	New lending from commercial banks	Bonds
1970	1362	447
1980	36231	1546
1982	39712	6208
1983	33588	2206
1984	29039	1787
1985	23954	7360
1986	21091	4866
1987	24334	4261
1988	24613	6432

[a] - The data applies to 111 countries that report to the World Bank Debtor Reporting System.

Sources: *World Bank* [1989b, 79].

In addition, intense domestic competition among banks, especially in the USA, an underdeveloped system of criteria to evaluate sovereign lending risks, and the belief of the existence in implicit guarantees by industrial countries in case of international financial emergencies[39] made the initially profitable less-industrialized country credit business appear attractive. Despite experiences of sovereign defaults in the past, the "sovereigns don't go bankrupt" illusion prevailed among bankers until the 1982 Mexican moratorium.

A number of reasons has been cited as contributing to the deterioration of less-industrialized countries' economic posture. A worldwide recession in 1979 and 1980 caused a decline in production which reduced demand for raw materials. Prices for raw materials decreased which hit particularly those countries that exhibited relatively little diversification of exports. The goal of balance-of-payments adjustment financing, however, could not be achieved as the majority of funds have been used for extending consumption expenditures, including government spending for noneconomic or inefficient purposes, in capital flight,

---

39 V. section 4.5.1.

and for other non-investive reasons. Interest rates moved up as a consequence of a restrictive US monetary policy in the inflationary period of the beginning of the 1980s. The floating rate mechanism used for international loans raised the absolute amount of debt service of the debtor countries. In 1982 the floating rate mechanism was used for 60% of the commercial bank debt outstanding to Latin American countries. In this year interest payments even exceeded principal repayments due. In 1987 it applied to 70% of Latin American debt (*Röller* [1987, 8]).

In the aftermath of the Mexican moratorium of August 1982 new bank lending to most less-industrialized and some Eastern European countries took the form of "involuntary lending". This term describes the need of commercial banks to mobilize and reschedule interest and principal repayments due by extending new loans. Such rescheduling agreements have so far averted an imminent collapse of the world financial system. Since 1986, the previously prevailing interpretation of the debt crisis of most rescheduling countries as a liquidity crisis was gradually given up. Instead, the impression surfaced that in the long run no valid prospects for complete or even orderly repayment by the most indebted countries exist. In the course of the debt crisis two political initiatives launched by the US government have received significant public attention.

3.1.2. The "Baker Plan"

The proposal by former US treasury secretary *Baker*, put forward at the annual meeting of the IMF and the World Bank in Seoul 1985, combined three elements. (cf. *Cline* [1987, 78]). First, it asked debtor countries to pursue growth oriented economic policies through undertaking major structural reforms aimed at reducing budget deficits, removing trade restrictions, denationalizing state enterprises, alleviating inflation and facilitating balance of payments adjustment.

Second, the role of the international institutions was underlined. Namely the World Bank should increase its efforts through extending the scope and effectiveness of its structural adjustment loans. It was suggested that the World Bank and the IADB increase disbursements to the major debtor countries between 1986 and 1988 from a projected US$ 6 billion p.a. to US$ 9 billion p.a. In addition, the catalytic function of the World Bank in stimulating "fresh money" commitments by commercial banks, i.e. lending of new funds not intended to reschedule old funds, through mechanisms like cofinancing should have been reinforced. The IFC and the MIGA should have been instrumental in attracting additional non-debt creating flows to these countries.

Third, it asked commercial banks to increase their lending to the 15 major debtor countries between 1986 and 1988 by US$ 20 billion to support their economic adjustment efforts. This implied a yearly growth rate of commercial bank lending to these countries of 2½% to 3%. Also, the banks should consider to lend to other countries with debt problems, should they arise. However, the major deficiency of the Baker Plan was the lack of the provision of an institutional framework for implementation of the promulgated measures. In addition, a tumbling oil price neutralized its effects on the prime target of the plan - Mexico (cf. *Gilbert* [1986, 45]).

3.1.3. The "Brady Plan"

After reconsideration of the failure of the Baker Plan and with the recognition that without some kind of debt reduction rescheduling countries would not be able to return to normal market relationships in March 1989 the new US treasury secretary *Brady* proposed a new conceptual framework for debt crisis management (cf. *Islam* [1989]). This Plan, for the first time, recognizes the institutional obstacles for commercial banks to accelerate the process of generating innovative transaction modes conducive to debt reduction. Debt reduction is increasingly viewed as a precondition for successful economic adjustment in the highly indebted countries (cf. *IIF* [1989, 21seqq.]).

As a major element it calls upon the IMF and the World Bank to support debt reduction by commercial banks through guarantees on the remaining portion of debt after an exchange of their old claims for lower principal instruments - utilizing the menu approach - or partial debt buy-backs. Both organizations have agreed to provide a total of US$ 25 billion over three years and Japan has committed US$ 4.5 billion for this purpose (*Sachs* [1989b, 88]). In addition, it is expected that industrial countries will reschedule bilateral official debt, provide new money to debtors pursuing debt reduction, follow sound economic policies, and in particular further liberalize their trade relations with rescheduling countries.

As a prerequisite for qualification for debt reduction, rescheduling countries would have to follow IMF and World Bank designed growth-oriented policies to increase domestic savings, promote foreign investment, and reverse capital flight. One important measure to enable large-scale debt reductions should be the negotiation of a temporary waiver of certain obstructive clauses contained in existing loan contracts[40]. Banks' domicile country governments should facilitate debt reduction by eliminating some regulatory barriers blocking banks' willingness to participate therein.

The return of flight capital is to be achieved by further extending debt equity swap programs in rescheduling countries to allow domestic investors to repatriate foreign holdings. Commercial banks are asked to provide new money in response to the public funding support for the respective debt reduction scheme and/or debt equity conversion opportunities. However, for successful implementation more operative details would need to be specified.

There are substantial difficulties, however, to implement any debt reduction plan. What criteria should be used to allocate the implied relief? Which countries should benefit? The principle of success (or incentive) compatibility would favor relief for middle-income countries which successfully conformed with prescribed adjustment programs and demonstrate prospects for further economic growth. The principle of failure (or poverty) compatibility would favor relief for the poorest countries with no prospects for future rehabilitation. If the latter principle is applied, this represents a disincentive for the more successsful country governments as in order to qualify for debt reduction a lowering of economic performance becomes attractive (cf. *Franke* [1990]). The setting of country-specific criteria for debt reduction would be the appropriate route but is obstructed by competition of debtor countries for external financing.

3.1.4. Three Stages of Debt Crisis Management

Parallel to the economic measures in managing the crisis, three stages can be distinguished from a legal perspective (*Reisner/Gruson/Thomas* [1988, 221seqq.]). A first phase, beginning with the onset of the crisis, was characterized by the need

---

40 V. section 3.2.3.

to develop some formal structure for enabling negotiations between sovereign debtors and several hundreds of bank creditors - a task with only very few precedents. The resulting fairly uniform framework provided for the involvement of the IMF, the debtor country's official creditors, and the commercial banks. In this period rescheduling countries' debts were catalogued and consolidated and only maturities coming due in the relatively near future were restructured.

In the second stage also medium-term maturities were rescheduled. These so-called multiyear restructuring agreements (MYRAs) - initiated with the 1984 Mexican rescheduling - generally included grace periods for the first years of the agreements, interest rate reductions, and lengthenings of amortization periods. The emphasis was put on restoring a borrower's debt service capacity for a period of up to 20 years. Hence, "fresh money" facilities were often included in the agreements to support a debtor's efforts in this respect. In addition, the adoption of a stabilization program proposed by the IMF, often accompanied by World Bank adjustment lending, was usually required from the debtor country government. New lending by the IMF and World Bank and by commercial banks was often made conditional upon each other.

Within these first two periods a couple of behavioral principles emerged as a consequence of the legal design of the relationships between creditors and between the creditors and the borrower. Certain covenants such as the negative pledge, the sharing, and the mandatory prepayment clause established an equality of treatment of creditors which, in effect, concentrated all originally independent credit contracts into one extensive package. Hence, all creditors now consented to be treated as a single entity and were thereby forced to act in unison. On the other hand, also all previously separate borrowers or at least all public sector borrowers in a particular rescheduling country were now treated as a single group.

Since 1985, a third stage of debt crisis management is characterized by the emergence of innovations that have led to a certain extent of disaggregation of the debt. This development increasingly obstructs the maintenance of the equal treatment-principle prevalent in the first two stages. These innovations included various swap schemes based upon trading opportunities offered by an growing secondary market for rescheduling country debt - i.e. in particular debt equity swaps and attempts to securitize existing claims. This development was causative for the application of the so-called "menu" approach in rescheduling negotiations which was formally instituted for the first time in the 1987 Argentine rescheduling.

3.1.5. The Menu Approach

The basic idea of the menu approach is to provide banks with an opportunity to select a financial product from a "menu of options" that closely corresponds to its particular needs. Transaction modes which may become part of a menu can be classified into two classes - debt restructuring and conversion options, and new lending options (cf. *Fischer* [1988, 184seq.]). Besides, traditional syndicated Eurolending fresh money instruments may comprise onlending, bonds, FRNs, interest capitalization, contingency financing, project loans, cofinancing, sale/leaseback, and certain trade financing schemes. Among new debt conversion modes are, debt equity swaps, debt for debt swaps, debt for commodity, nature, and development swaps as well as debt buy-backs (cf. *Berger* [1988, 125seq.] and *Fischer* [1988, 186seq.])[41]. Table 3 is intended to provide an impression of the multitude of menu elements.

---

41 In late 1988 a menu approach was also applied to official credit relationships between sovereign creditors of the Paris Club and seven African debtor countries. Elements of this menu are (1) partial cancellation of debt, (2) extended maturities, and (3) concessional interest rates (*IMF Survey* [1989, 103]).

Table 3: Elements of the Menu of Options Used by Commercial Banks

RESTRUCTURING AND CONVERSION OPTIONS

- Traditional syndicated floating rate Euroloans
- Debt Conversion
  - Debt equity swap
    - Company-specific investment
    - Investment in conversion fund
- Debt for debt swap
    - Relending
    - Currency redenomination
    - Interest rate redenomination
    - Debt for bond swap
      - Debt for "regular" bond swap
      - Debt for exit bond swap
    - Debt for FRN swap
    - Debt for local currency swap
- Debt for commodity swap
- Debt for nature swap
- Debt for development swap
- Debt buy-backs

NEW LENDING OPTIONS

- Traditional syndicated floating rate Euroloans
- Onlending
- New money bonds
  - "Regular" bonds
  - Exit bonds
- New money FRNs
- Interest Capitalization
- Contingency financing
- Project lending
- Cofinancing
- Sale/leaseback schemes
- Trade financing schemes
  - Export prefinancing
  - Medium term revolving trade financing facility

Whereas some of the innovative swap schemes mentioned in table 3 had initially been used independently of the specifications of rescheduling agreements, it has gradually become necessary to make their realization compatible with these agreements. This is because they often cause conflicts with those contractual clauses that are intended to establish equality of treatment of creditors. Therefore, new clauses have been included in rescheduling agreements to provide for implementation of these innovations - giving rise to the use of the metaphor menu (cf. *Messer* [1989, 68seq.]).

3.2. INSTITUTIONAL BACKGROUND OF INNOVATIONS IN INTERNATIONAL DEBT MANAGEMENT

The development outlined in the preceding section evolved on the basis of a particular set of institutional features of the original product - the customary and legally stipulated rules involved in syndicated bank lending to less-industrialized countries and rescheduling. The most important of these features are described below.

3.2.1. The Syndication Mechanism

Syndication[42] is a credit transaction mode that effectively reduces transaction costs for both the borrower and the lender as through syndication the total amount of a single loan transaction is increased by bundling a number of creditor banks - in the case of sovereign lending sometimes several hundred. This is reflected in the terms of syndicated credits. Generally one bank acts as the "agent", i.e. it administrates the disbursement and collection of loan principal and interest payments which reduces set-up and participation costs. The agent function is usually taken on by the "lead manager" of a syndicated loan, who together with other "managers" evaluates market conditions, negotiates the loan terms, and organizes the commitment of loan funds by the managing and the other "participating banks". Again this teaming is a measure to reduce transaction costs. Banks participating in syndicated Eurocredit lending may broadly be distinguished into three classes: (1) global banks, (2) medium-sized banks or niche players, and (3) small banks.

The legal design of syndicated loan contracts is determined by three institutionalized types of clauses (*Bucheit/Reisner* [1988, 501]). One delineates the relationships of the syndicate members to the borrower. Another type regulates the relationships of the agent bank and sometimes the managers to the other syndicate members. The third type applies to the relationships between the lending

---

[42] A very detailed treatment of syndicated lending is provided by *McDonald* [1982].

banks and is intended to institutionalize cooperation among them. This last category increasingly impedes the implementation of restructurings from the outset of the third stage of the debt management process because of divergent interests of many different banks. It is dealt with in more detail in section 3.2.3.

As in the case of sovereign borrowing the majority of banks participating in a syndicate do not possess the same extensive country reporting and risk evaluation systems as the larger banks of the management group, those banks that are not represented in the management group relied more and more on the analysis of the managers (cf. *Park/Zwick* [1985, 104]). In principle, however, the responsibility for careful credit analysis rests with each individual member of the syndicate.

3.2.2. Specifics of the Rescheduling Process

The reasons for the emergence of large-scale debt reschedulings are manyfold and to a large extent the same as for the debt crisis itself. The long period of high interest rates from 1979 to 1985 and the persevering recession resulting from the second oil-price shock has been the underlying economic setting. As the respective loan contracts usually involved floating interest rates debt service obligations increased - largely independent from conditions in debtor countries. The more specific reasons why a sovereign debtor may become unable to service its debts are (*Finance & Development* [1983, 26]):

- Its total debt service obligations exceed its capacity to pay because of excessive borrowing;

- the maturity structure of its total debt may lead to an accumulation of debt service obligations at a certain date;

- the management of its balance of payments may have been inadequate in order to continue debt service;

- substantial drops in certain commodities prices or natural disasters may significantly reduce export earnings and, thus, its ability to pay.

A very important reason why reschedulings have been preferred to the acceptance of actual defaults has been the financial vulnerability of large bank lenders, particularly in the USA. Acceptance of default would have caused bankruptcy of some major international banks with unpredictable repercussions on the global financial system. However, institutional conditions significantly determined the course and design of particular debt restructuring exercises.

One such reason for the development of the rescheduling mechanism as an alternative to outright default has been the emergence of contractual innovations such as particularly the cross-default clause[43] which effectively raises the cost of default for the borrower (cf. *Folkerts-Landau* [1985, 325seqq.]). The syndication of loans similarly aggregates the responsibility among lenders and, thus, institutionalizes cooperation among them. Syndication, therefore, enhances the effectiveness of such contractual clauses because all bank lenders would be affected by a default.

In fact, a rescheduling is a measure to prevent the declaration of a de jure default although a technical default is apparent. A de jure default is not desirable because of higher costs involved for the borrower and the lender. Such costs arise for the debtor from the expected suspension of any significant access to international financial markets. For banks a de jure default could imply the bankruptcy of one or a few large commercial banks, particularly in the USA, with unpredictable consequences for the world financial system.

The forum for the renegotiation of credit relationships between governments, i.e. official debt, is the Paris Club, in which a debtor country presents its case to representatives of the 17 governments of the DAC of the OECD, before bilateral agreements are drafted with each individual debtor. The framework for commercial bank reschedulings is not as formalized[44]. Loans arranged through syndicates of banks are renegotiated between the debtor and a bank steering committee[45] which is a group of experienced specialists from some 10 to 15 major banks often representing many hundreds of banks involved as creditors. Originally,

---

43 V. section 3.2.3.1.

44 Sometimes commercial banks involved in rescheduling negotiations are referred to as the "London Club".

45 Other terms used include "bank advisory group" and "bank working committee".

the majority of these loans have been for general purpose use and had not been tied to a use in specific companies or projects.

A particular rescheduling exercise usually starts with the sovereign borrower's notification of all creditors that he has to suspend payments because of the perception of an inability to pay. The debtor will formally request a rescheduling of the debt owed after a certain cut-off date. The rescheduling then takes the form of an explicit contractual agreement between all lenders and the sovereign borrower to modify the repayment schedule for principal and/or interest. The agreement has to cover all different debt categories concerned and their maturities. In case new funds ("fresh money"), independent of previous credits, shall be extended, their form and conditions have to be specified. The applicable interest rates, maturities, grace periods, and currency denominations have to be determined for both the previous and the new debt. Events of default, positive and negative covenants of the contract may have to be redefined. Finally, rescheduling fees and expenses have to be settled.

A good example of a traditional rescheduling is the 1984 Mexican commercial bank debt rescheduling of US$ 48.7 billion - the largest single restructuring until that time. It contained three parts: a partial prepayment and amendment of a US$ 56 billion credit agreement from 1983, a multi-year rescheduling of approximately US$ 20.1 billion of public sector debt originally falling due between 1985 and 1990, and the extension of maturities falling due between 1987 and 1990 under the then existing rescheduling agreements for debt which originally would have matured between 1982 and 1984 (cf. *Routledge* [1985, 164]).

The magnitude of sovereign debt reschedulings in the recent past is demonstrated by table 4.

Table 4: Multilateral Debt Rescheduling Agreements with Commercial Banks 1982-1989 (US$ million)

Item	1982-85	1986	1987	1988	1989
Number of agreements	18	12	19	10	4
Amounts restructured (US$billions)	42.0	72.7	89.7	79.7	n.a.
Average consolidation period (years)	2	2.8	4	6.6	n.a.
Average repayment terms:					
Maturity (years)	9	10	15	19	n.a.
Grace period (years)	4	4	5	7	n.a.
Spread over LIBOR (percent)	1.8	1.3	1	0.8	n.a.

Note: Agreements here represent agreements in principle with bank advisory committees as opposed to agreements signed. Often there is a substantial lag between an agreement in principle and actual signature.

Source: *World Bank* [1989b, 59].

Rescheduling agreements are usually much more complex and stringent than original loan agreements with regard to the application of several clauses, i.e. the governing law will be a foreign one, disputes will have to be settled in foreign courts, an extensive sovereign immunity waiver will be applied, and foreign exchange and other international monetary assets may have to be centralized with the central bank (*Wood* [1984, 134seq.]). However, the sequestration or attachement of borrowers' external assets which is to be facilitated by these measures, has rarely been adopted. As in the case of the freezing of Iranian assets, this action only applies to situations where the debtor displays hostile intent.

In order to fight inflation, stimulate internal economic growth and prevent rapid depletion of foreign exchange reserves of debtor countries a couple of measures have been attached to or paralleled rescheduling exercises. Often, particularly when they encompass the extension of fresh money loans, restructuring agreements include the provision that also the IMF should advance new money. This usually implies that the borrower would have to agree to an IMF austerity program. By applying this measure banks want to assure themselves of an adequate management of the debtor's economy.

On the other hand, also the IMF may ask banks to provide new funds as a condition for its loans (cf. *Wellons* [1985, 142seq]). Some restructuring agreements included currency redenomination options for non US banks, which allow these banks to convert all or only part of their renegotiated loans into loans denominated in their home currencies at prevailing market exchange rates and interest rates (cf. *Morgan Guaranty* [1984]). This measure can increase the weighted average maturity, or the duration of loan payments, which in turn alleviates the borrower's liquidity constraints.

However, as economic conditions in most debtor countries did not improve as desired and reschedulings took on an almost normal, self-evident character, banks have increasingly given in on some of their previously more stringent provisions. They have granted longer grace periods and have reduced spreads. See table 4 for an overview of the evolution of rescheduling conditions.

Representatives of US banks have chaired most steering committees in reschedulings because of the relatively higher exposures of US banks, particularly in Latin American debtor countries. Therefore they have also been dominant in devising the course of the rescheduling process - namely the continued extension of new loans. This course had been necessitated by the respective US institutional determinants applicable to non-performing loans, in particular the ninety-day rule which required banks to receive interest payments at regular intervals of 90 days in order to avoid the recognition of cutbacks in earnings (cf. *Williamson, M.L.* [1988, 19seq.])[46].

The increasing complexity of international loan and rescheduling agreements led to a growing involvement of legal experts. A few international law firms have created large specialized teams for legal consulting and the design of respective contracts. Although the transaction costs of legal services parties to the contract have to bear are not negligible it does not seem to be a valid conjecture that law firms have incentives to design contracts in such a way that future rendering of specialized legal services is not obstructed.

3.2.3. Important Contractual Provisions

Any innovation necessarily has to emerge from some pre-existing institutional structure. In international credit relationships a major element of this structure are the contracts which formally specify the rights and duties of contracting parties. A couple of clauses that are typical of almost all credit relationships between

46 Described in more detail in section 4.1.1.7.

commercial banks and less-industrialized countries have established a set of behavioral constraints that have created what *Buchheit/Reisner* [1988, 494] call an "uneasy confederation". That is, the application of these clauses in the course of the debt management process has - in concert - led to a uniformity of treatment of all creditor banks that did not prevail at the outset of the crisis and is increasingly viewed by many banks as a rather annoying impediment for the pursuit of individual strategies as will be shown in chapter 5.

However, these clauses fulfilled important functions at the onset of less-industrialized country lending when it was necessary to entice a large number of banks to participate in large-amount syndicated loan agreements. They had been designed to reduce the costs of enforcement of claims jointly held by hundreds of banks in particular to prevent smaller banks from free riding behavior.

The changing scope of application of these clauses and its resulting effect on the relationships among creditors is treated by *Buchheit/Reisner* [1988]. An understanding of the effect of these clauses on the creation of a strong mutual dependence of all creditors of a debtor country is important because this phenomenon is in stark contrast to the divergence of interests among commercial bank lenders which is caused by differing regulatory, tax, and accounting provisions in domicile countries as well as by political considerations and by their individual strategies[47,48]. In the following the most relevant clauses in this respect are described.

3.2.3.1. Cross-Default Clause

The cross-default clause stipulates a default on a particular loan whenever any separate entity included in the specification of the borrower, i.e. different government agencies or corporations, defaults on another loan. The definition of the conditions necessary for the assumption of a default are contained in events of default clauses. The clause serves the interest of the lender in that it prevents

---

47 In new money agreements such mutual dependence has also been established with official lenders like the IMF or industrial country governments by making these agreements conditional on according agreements with commercial banks and other tie-ins.

48 The following description relies primarily on *UNCTC* [1983] and *Bucheit/Reisner* [1988]. V. also *Messer* [1989, 39seqq.].

preferred treatment of other lenders by pursuing legal remedies against the debtor in case of a default[49].

Whereas in the pre-restructuring period the specification of which economic entities are included in the definition of the borrower has been fairly narrow, in the course of various restructuring exercises the umbrella-like character of these agreements led to an extension of this definition to include virtually all public companies and agencies of a particular debtor country. This not only led to a greater sensitivity to the occurence of a default with more farreaching implications for the borrower, i.e. increasing its default costs, but also extended the bond between all banks with exposure to this country. Thus it is a measure intended to reduce participation and information costs, in conjunction with the events of default clause particularly those of state verification. This is because it reduces potential conflicts between borrower and creditors over the question whether and when a default has ocurred.

Mitigations of harshly formulated cross-default clauses can be achieved by materiality tests and grace periods. This can f.i. be achieved by providing that a cross-default cannot be declared if a creditor of a loan in default waives the deficiency that would trigger the declaration of cross-default. Also, if some loan agreements specify grace periods, it can be provided that a default on the agreement in question cannot be declared until after the grace period for payment in the agreement that would trigger the cross-default clause had lapsed (*UNCTC* [1983, 65]).

3.2.3.2. Pari Passu Clause

The function of the pari passu clause is to insure at least equal rank of one loan agreement with other unsecured obligations and liabilities. Thus, it is designed to prevent the incurrence by the borrower of any future debt of senior status and to prevent the subordination of new debt under existing debt of the borrower in the first place. This clause, therefore, is intended to prevent modification costs arising from contractual adaptation. This may be necessary when debt service

---

49 Events of default clauses specify exactly what events give rise to triggering a default. Cf. *Messer* [1989, 43seqq.].

irregularities on subordinated debt occur f.i. as a consequence of a deterioration of the debtor's servicing capacity.

3.2.3.3. Negative Pledge Clause

The negative pledge clause provides that no liens are created or allowed on the property or revenues by the obligor or guarantor that could impair the prospects of other unsecured lenders to be serviced or otherwise satisfied. It complements the pari passu clause as it also prevents the borrower from creating seniority for other existing and future debt. It thereby contributes to the parity of treatment of all lenders and should also serve to save on modification costs.

The broader the definition of the borrower, the more likely it is that the combined specifications of the negative pledge clause and the cross-default clause could trigger an event of default. During the restructuring process this definition has extented to include all public sector entities, the number of which may be very large. Therefore, appropriate exceptions from the negative pledge clause have often been applied. These are intended to better reflect both the interests of the lenders and the borrower not to cause precipitate reactions to insignificant events and to insure that different treatment of private and official creditors - where desirable - is possible (cf. *Bradfield/Jacklin* [1984, 136]).

3.2.3.4. Sharing Clause

Sharing provisions ensure that no creditor of a particular rescheduling agreement can enjoy preferred treatment in receiving payments or other assets from the debtor. Pro rata sharing between all creditors of any payments received is stipulated. Should any lender receive such payments, he is required to transfer the respective amount to the agent bank which will distribute it among all creditors according to their proportionate exposure under the agreement in question. Thus, this clause also contributes to the sharing of risks of non-payment among all creditors and thereby also reduces modification costs.

3.2.3.5. Mandatory Prepayment Clause

Should a borrower repay debts incurred under a particular credit contract prior to their specified due date, he is obliged to prepay all lenders on a ratable basis. Whereas sharing clauses regulate the payment positions of lenders under the same agreement, mandatory prepayment clauses serve to assure creditors under one agreement that the debtor will not give priority to lenders under another agreement by means of prepayment. Again, modification cost reduction is the underlying economic rationale as a sharing of the risk of non-payment is achieved. More recently, mandatory prepayment clauses are often drafted so as to cover prepayments in foreign currency only. This helps not to prevent opportunities to reduce foreign currency debt by means of domestic currency repayments as may be possible with debt conversion modes like f.i. debt equity swaps (*Buchheit/Reisner* [1988, 512]).

3.2.3.6. Other Clauses

Another important provision to be found in international syndicated loan contracts is the most favored debt clause (cf. *Wood* [1984, 138]). This provision requires that the debtor has to enter into comparable arrangements for other debt before a particular rescheduling agreement comes into force. This clause may possibly demand that these obligations, which may include trade and securitized debt, may not be serviced on more favorable terms. Amendment or contractual change clauses specify which clauses can be modified or replaced under what conditions. This reduces participation and modification costs. Usually, in case of the alteration of maturity or the reduction of principal or interest claims unanimous approval by all creditors is required[50].

Also, most syndicated loan agreements contain clauses that specify the procedures and conditions for the transfer of debt[51]. These are relevant for the trading of loans in the secondary market. Some of the more recent debt agreements contain special debt exchange provisions like assignment, participation, and transfer certificate clauses (cf. *Messer* [1989, 49seqq.] and *Wulfken/Berger* [1988b, 354]). These specify those categories of debt and rights based thereupon that may become subject of an exchange of debt, the types of other assets allowed in the exchange, the types of persons entitled to engage in the exchange, and other conditions of the exchange. In addition, such provisions may exempt the respective

---

50 V. *Messer* [1989, 69seq.]

51 V. section 3.3.1.3.

debt from the implications of the sharing and mandatory prepayment clauses (cf. *Chamberlin/Gruson/Weltchek* [1988, 420seqq.]).

In contrast to domestic loan contracts, international loan contracts with sovereign borrowers are much less stringent in the scope and type of the information the debtor is required to report to the creditors. *Bucheit/Reisner* [1988, 495seq.] view this relative lack of reporting requirements as a reflection of the "sovereigns never go bankrupt" fiction shared by many bankers and industrialized country regulators.

3.3. RECENT INNOVATIONS

In the course of the debt management process attention has focused more and more on ways to redesign the contractual relationships into forms that allow better allocations of risk for participating banks and also provide opportunities for some to exit these relationships altogether. The most important organizational innovation that has evolved during this time is the secondary market for rescheduling country debt. On the basis of the possibility to trade non-securitized assets with a discount from face-value, various new transaction modes emerged which allow the transformation of claims. Among these, debt equity swaps are the most acclaimed. Debt equity swaps also form part of the so-called "menu of options" for commercial banks.

3.3.1. The Secondary Market for Rescheduling Country Debt

3.3.1.1. Participants

A secondary market for rescheduling country loans emerged already as early as 1980 (*Finneran* [1987, 28]). New York and London are the main trading centers. Besides commercial banks, multinational corporations participate in the market as buyers of loans to countries where they have identified investment opportunities. Finally, investment banks and brokers take part as market makers, consultants and intermediaries. The number of participants can be estimated at 300 and is increasing (*Lerbinger* [1987, 599]).

Brokers act as go-between for buyers and sellers of loans by identifying appropriate counterparties and by consulting the parties in all aspects of the realization of a trade. On the other hand, they trade on their own account for generating profits from arbitrage (back-to-back transaction) and in order to put together complex debt equity conversions that require the combination of a variety of loans in separate trades (*Nicolaides* [1987, 116]). Thereby brokers contribute to increase the liquidity of the market. Their profit takes the form of fees or spreads.

3.3.1.2. Transaction Modes

A number of different transaction modes exist (*Lerbinger* [1987, 597seq.])[52]. The simplest form is the loan sale or cash swap which consists of a transfer of the claim to the buyer for a cash payment of a negotiated price. A loan swap is the transfer of one claim to the buyer for the transfer of another claim - usually on a different debtor country - to the seller. Differences in negotiated prices are compensated through supplementary cash payments. If no cash payment is involved in a loan swap, it is called a ratio swap. A ratio swap presupposes identity of negotiated values of the traded claims at the time of the trade. The face values do not need to correspond to each other. If face values are equal but negotiated prices are not, a loan swap is called a par swap. Other financial claims like Euronotes or floating rate notes are also used as payment in trading rescheduling country loans.

3.3.1.3. Legal Institutions

For the actual transfer of specific claims three contractual forms are legally institutionalized[53]. As New York law is most often chosen for international loan contracts, the following description of transfer modes is primarily based on New York law. English law implications are alluded to as well as the loan contracts of a few rescheduling countries are governed by English law[54].

---

52 For case examples of these various transaction modes v. *Messer* [1989, 91seqq.]. An account of the procedural details for their effectuation can be found *ibid.* [135seqq.].

53 The following brief overview of transfer modes draws heavily on the much more detailed treatment in *Wulfken/Berger* [1988].

54 Also French law applies to loan contracts of a few debtor countries, particularly in Africa. However, for the vast majority of rescheduling countries mainly New York law and - less so - English law are relevant.

3.3.1.3.1. Novation

A novation is a contract in which the old creditor is completely substituted by a new creditor who was not previously a party to the contract. The old contract is terminated and a new contract with exactly the same content is created which implies that all rights and duties of the old creditor are transferred to the new one. Therefore, a novation requires consent of all parties involved in the contractual relationship (*American Law Institute* [1981, § 280]). A novation is also possible under English law (cf. *Cheshire/Fifoot/Furmston* [1986, 509] and *Treitel* [1987, 498]).

3.3.1.3.2. Assignment

The assignment is the second legal conduit for transferring sovereign debt. Here, the transfer only involves a certain right, i.e. primarily the right to receive interest and repayment of principal. However, the assignor remains party to the contract. The assignee obtains a right from him which is legally enforceable against the sovereign debtor. The assignor generally keeps all remaining duties (*American Law Institute* [1981, § 317]).

It is not necessary in principle to issue a notification to the debtor for an assignment to become effective. Hence, many international loan contracts contain a clause that requires such notification in case an assignment is intended as sovereign borrowers often want to stay aware of the composition of the creditors' syndicate. Also, contracts may even prohibit assignments. However, under New York law there are some restrictions concerning the validity of such prohibitions of assignments (cf. *American Law Institute* [1981, § 322 (2) (b)] and *Calamari/Perillo* [1977, 648]). An assignment that is executed despite of a contractual prohibition remains effective but gives rise to claims for damages.

Under English law, assignments can take one of two forms. A legal assignment provides the assignee with a direct enforcable claim on the debtor. For a legal assignment to become effective, several conditions have to be met (*Treitel* [1987, 506seq.]). Furthermore, a significant cost factor is introduced as 1% of the transaction amount is taxable after the Stamp Act 1891 (cf. *Hughes/Palache* [1984, 22]).

An informal assignment which does not conform to the conditions for a legal assignment may become valid as an equitable assignment. Equitable assignments do neither require any notification to the borrower nor any written form. Also, they do not need to be absolute, i.e. also partial claims can be assigned and the actual transfer can be made contingent upon certain conditions. On the other hand, an equitable assignment does not provide the assignee with any right that would be enforceable on his behalf.

3.3.1.3.3. Participation

The third transfer mechanism is the participation. Here the old creditor transfers a separate sub-participation of the full or a partial amount of the respective loan to another creditor, i.e. the participant. The participant acquires the right to receive the total or a portion of all payments of interest and principal repayments for paying a specified price. The old creditor remains party to the contract and collects the borrower's payments; the contractual relationship between the borrower and the old creditor is not affected by the participation. The participant's claims are directed solely against the old creditor. Usually the existence of such claims are not indicated to the borrower. Although under English law - like under New York law - a participation does not represent a legally defined contractual form, transactions of the same kind are possible.

3.3.1.4. Volume and Pricing

The volume of transactions in the secondary market grew from approximately US$ 1 billion in 1981 to an estimated US$ 50 billion in 1989[55]. Relative to the amount of all outstanding bank debt to severely indebted middle-income countries of about US$ 396 billion in 1988[56] these figures demonstrate the lack of liquidity of the market (*Finneran* [1987, 28], *Evans* [1988, 25]). Exact data of secondary market activity is not available as most transactions are not officially recorded. Debt of about 35 countries is offered in the market (*Lerbinger* [1987, 599]). Two segments can be distinguished. One consists of frequently traded debt (approximately from 20 countries, of which the majority are Latin American), the other consists of debt

---

55 Based on information from market participants. Double counting of transactions makes these figures somewhat vague.

56 Cf. table 1 on p. 2.

that is only rarely traded. Discounts on face values of transferred loans range between 50% and 90%. Figure 4 depicts the development of average secondary market loan prices in 1988 and 1989.

Figure 4: Secondary Market Pricing of Rescheduling Country Loans, January 1988-September 1989 (percentage of face value)

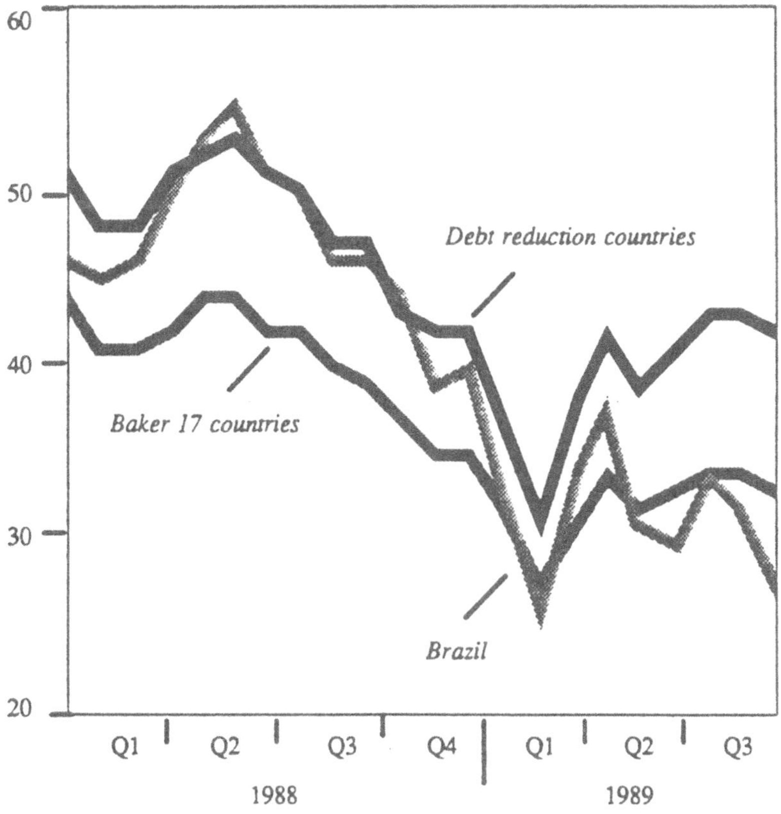

Note: Baker 17 countries comprise Argentina, Bolivia, Brazil, Chile, Colombia, Costa Rica, Cote d'Ivoire, Ecuador, Jamaica, Mexico, Morocco, Nigeria, Peru, Philippines, Uruguay, Venezuela, and Yugoslavia.
Debt reduction countries comprise countries expected to participate in debt reduction operations such as Mexico and the Philippines.

Source: *World Bank* [1989b, 18].

The marked gradual decrease in secondary market prices reflects the fact that supply has exceeded demand for the most part. A factor explaining some significant price increases is the introduction of debt equity swap programs by some rescheduling countries which tends to stimulate demand. On the other hand prices dropped substantially after the 1987 decision by major US banks to increase their loan loss provisions and continue to do so as a consequence of further capital increases of banks (cf. *Faria/Stott/Buchanan* [1988]).

As is true for any market transaction, the prices emerge from negotiated deals which often take account of very specific interests of the trading partners. However, a distinction of this market lies in the degree of difference of these interests and its lack of liquidity which both result in relatively volatile prices. For a bank engaged in a trade, its particular cost structure may include elements that represent relative disadvantages compared to other banks. Institutional determinants - supervisory, tax, and accounting regulations - and bank-specific conditions, like, for instance, liquidity preference, provisioning capacity, cross-selling potential, and future business interests, play a significant role in the valuation process[57]. Hence, a loan manager at one bank may accept a higher discount than a manager at another bank. Expectations about the future income effects of the claim in question are dominated by expectations of portfolio consequences.

Furthermore, the various claims traded often differ substantially depending on whether they are eligible or ineligible for debt equity swap programs, whether in case of public debt it is rescheduled debt or fresh money debt, whether it is bank or non-bank debt, and what the identity of the debtor is. Also private sector debt prices vary according to whether the debt is included or excluded from reschedulings, whether it is securitized, or whether the debtor is a bank (cf. *Faria/Stott/Buchanan* [1988]). Thus, there exist no "official" prices of quasi-homogeneous paper. This and the relative lack of liquidity, which is partially a reflection of the market's unofficial character, result in substantial fluctuations of prices. This is because relatively insignificant amounts of single transactions can lead to substantial price changes.

Prices published by market-making investment banks are therefore merely indicators for the potential valuation of a future transaction. Although these prices may help transacting parties to establish a base for negotiations, they are clearly

---

57 Cf. section 4.4.

not good indicators of the value of a specific claim. This impression stems partly from market makers' practice not to give detailed account of specific transactions but to quote negotiated discounts on a per country basis only - a measure that also serves as a marketing tool.

Little price differentiation among rescheduling countries with perceived differences in debt service capacity is observed. Thus, also the US regulatory agencies have come to view secondary market prices more as indicators of short-term supply than of the ultimate value of loans over the medium- to long-term (*OCC/FRB/FDIC* [1989a, 25]). To insulate debt equity investors from the market's price volatility, in 1988 some banks have introduced to offer options to buy or sell debt eligible for conversions (*Faria/Stott/Buchanan* [1988]).

3.3.2. Debt Reduction Modes

The existence of a secondary market for rescheduling country debt which allows a valuation of claims lower than face value gave rise to opportunities for the conversion of loans into other assets or rights. The conversion usually implies some degree of reduction of external debt from the perspective of the debtor country. According to *OCC/FRB/FDIC* [1989a, 16] conversions of rescheduling country debt through various swapping schemes and debt settlements has amounted to more than US$ 20 billion of the face value of commercial bank debt in 1987 and 1988. The *World Bank* provides the following data.

Table 5: Rescheduling Country Debt Conversions 1984-1988 (US$ millions)

Conversion mode	1984	1985	1986	1987	1988
Debt equity swaps	773	1843	1522	3335	9205
Exit bonds	0	0	0	15	4725
Buy-backs	0	0	0	0	648
Informal[a]	0	0	0	3500	5414
Other	0	245	714	1337	2366
Total	**773**	**2088**	**2236**	**8188**	**22358**
All transactions[b]	2000	4000	7000	12000	50000

[a] - Informal conversions by private citizens and companies taking place outside of official programs.
[b] - Includes all conversions and asset trades on the secondary market.

Source: *World Bank* [1989b, 18].

3.3.2.1. Debt Equity Swaps

The possibility to sell debt with a discount and, thus, to buy a certain nominal claim for a price below face value led to the emergence of debt equity swaps[58]. This transaction mode allows the buyer to use the purchased claim for conversion into debtor country currency equity investments - either as direct or portfolio investment.

The first step usually consists of the transfer via the secondary market of a specific loan from a creditor bank to an interested investor - usually a multinational corporation. However, in a direct swap the original bank creditor may himself take the role of the investor. The investor then presents this claim to the central bank of the debtor country for conversion of the face value of the loan into local currency. Besides the levying of taxes, in most cases another discount is deducted by the central bank from the face value of the presented claim, which is lower than the secondary market discount.

Factors that influence the ultimate financial cost of a debt equity swap transaction to the investor, are the purchase price of the original loan, the local currency purchase price of the equity investment, the discount and other deductions levied by the debtor country, the exchange rate and fees payable to an intermediary for the arrangement of the transaction[59].

Hence, with debt equity conversions the investor can take advantage of a preferential exchange rate for his investment. Most rescheduling countries, however, have limited debt equity swap investment opportunities to certain industrial sectors and/or categories of debt. In some countries, specialized mutual fund-type conversion funds have been set up for debt equity investors that allow to invest somewhat smaller amounts and benefit from greater risk diversification and expert fund management[60]. In order to complete one debt equity swap transaction it is often necessary to combine a number of asset trades in order to arrive at the

---

58 For detailed treatments of debt equity swaps v. *Rubin* [1987] and *Wulfken* [1989].

59 For an economic analysis of debt equity swaps v. *Franke* [1989a].

60 For further reference v. *Roth* [1989] and *Berger* [1988, 128].

required amount of the investment. This task is usually performed by an investment bank. Since 1984 the emergence of debt equity swaps has substantially spurred secondary market activity.

Table 6: Volume of Debt Equity Swap Transactions in Selected Debtor Countries (US$ billions)[a]

Country	Cumulative 1983-88	Percent of end-1985 debt to commercial banks
Argentina	1.32	5
Bolivia	0.06	10
Brazil	5.89	8
Chile	2.35	16
Mexico	2.40	3
Nigeria	0.04	1
Philippines	0.53	4
Venezuela	0.35	1
Total	**12.94**	**5**

[a] - Excludes conversions outside formal programs.

Source: *Morgan Guaranty* [1988, 7].

Besides debt equity swaps other transaction modes for debt conversion have been employed.

3.3.2.2. Debt for Debt Swaps

Debt for debt swaps consist of the exchange of the old debt instrument into a new debt instrument. Here, a distinction has to be made between conversions exercised as part of a rescheduling agreement by the original borrowers and conversions that are undertaken after purchase of a loan in the secondary market. In the first case conversion can take the form of securitization of rescheduling country debt, i.e. the substitution of a loan by a negotiable debt instrument, like for instance a floating rate note (debt for FRN Swap), or a bond (debt for bond swap). Also, the execution of interest rate and currency switching options can be categorized as debt for debt swap transactions.

Bonds used in debt for bond swaps usually consist of low-interest bonds with long maturities[61]. If the new bond implies the eventual exemption of the respective claimant from future fresh money commitments and reschedulings, these bonds are called "exit bonds". The concept of the exit bond can also be used for new money lending. Exit bonds can be distinguished in those that provide concessions to the borrower in terms of the interest rate or in terms of the value of the bond issue (cf. *Williamson, J.* [1988, 22]). The validity of an exit bond issue depends on either the existence of some form of collateral or the introduction of seniority or guarantees. This transaction mode has so far only been implemented in Argentina, Mexico, and Venezuela with limited success. The implementation in Mexico was only made possible by collateralizing the bonds with US Treasury zero-bonds (*Ebenroth/Cremer* [1988]).

An example for secondary market-based debt for debt conversions are debt for local currency swaps. Here, a local investor exchanges a foreign currency claim bought in the secondary market into a local currency debt instrument issued by the respective debtor country central bank.

3.3.2.3. Debt Buy-Backs

Partial debt repurchases result in the elimination of a share of existing obligations through a mere buy-back at a discount by the debtor. Total debt repurchases have not ocurred to this date. This can either be a direct transaction negotiated by all contracting parties as part of an official agreement or it can be an indirect transaction based on secondary market transactions conducted by the debtor. Besides buy-backs by private and public sector companies, buy-backs by governments have been adopted in the cases of Bolivia, Chile, Mexico, and Peru (*IMF* [1989, 39]). However, in total amounts, application of this debt reduction mode has been rather limited so far, as in the case of buy-backs financed by debtor country resources creditors have insisted on using existing foreign exchange for

---

61 In the most prominent case of a debt for bond swap the Mexican government issued US$ 10 billion of 20 year bonds with an interest rate spread of $1^{5}/8\%$ over LIBOR p.a. in exchange for US$ 14.3 billion of old debt at $^{13}/16\%$ over LIBOR p.a. For a detailed analysis of this transaction v. *Ebenroth/Cremer* [1988].

servicing existing obligations and have feared new money funds could simply be used to finance buy-backs, causing a loss for participating banks in return.

3.3.2.4. Debt for Nature Swaps

Since 1987 significant public attention has been received by so-called debt for nature swaps or debt for environment swaps. In view of the continuing clearing of large areas of rain forest in many highly indebted countries and the threat this development poses to human life on earth through its effects on the world climate, i.e. its contribution to the so-called green-house effect, and the consequential obliteration of a multitude of biological species, any possible means of preventing this process to continue deserves special consideration (cf. *Oberndörfer* [1989]).

The prevention of substantial further destruction of natural habitats in less-industrialized countries has also evolved as a major motivating factor for debt reduction. The idea is that only by relieving the debtor countries from the constraining financial effects of over-indebtedness can they pursue ecologically sound policies which are perceived to be of increasing urgency[62].

A debt for nature swap consists of a donation of rescheduling country debt to or a purchase of such debt on the secondary market by some conservation organization which exchanges the debt - either the face value or the face value minus a discount - at the central bank of the respective country into local currency. Contractual provisions require the use of the funds exchanged for investment in governmentally approved environmental protection and/or conservation measures[63].

3.3.2.5. Debt for Development Swaps

Similar to debt for nature swaps, debt for development swaps involve the obtainment of a particular rescheduling country's debt from the creditor bank -

---

62 This is the conclusion of a statement of principles on the protection of tropical rain forests by the Commission of the European Community (*FAZ* [1. August 1989]).

63 For detailed treatments v. *Hansen* [1989] and *Chamberlin/Gruson/Weltchek* [1988, 440seqq.]. Debt for nature swaps have been conducted in Bolivia, Ecuador, Costa Rica, and in the Philippines (*ibid.*).

either by means of a donation or a secondary market transaction - and subsequent conversion into local currency. The funds are then used in financing specific development projects in the respective debtor country. Administration of the transaction and subsequent implementation of projects is conducted by some local not-for-profit organization associated with a not-for-profit organization in the bank's domicile country.

3.3.2.6. Debt for Commodity Swaps

This transaction mode, also termed debt for export, debt for goods, or debt for products swap, is intended to liquidate a particular claim against a rescheduling country creditor through the sale of goods or services provided by the respective rescheduling country. Usually a creditor bank will agree to market a selection of a country's goods and will use part of the proceeds to cancel the bank's loan exposure. The remaining part will be reverted to the debtor country in cash. Although the amounts of debt swapped have been insignificant, the most successful program of this kind has been implemented in Peru (cf. *Chamberlin/Gruson/Weltchek* [1988, 457seq.]). Also in various other countries like Brazil, Sudan and Bolivia export transactions involving rescheduling country debt have been conducted sporadically (*Schubert* [1987, 41]).

4. INSTITUTIONAL DETERMINANTS OF INNOVATIONS IN INTERNATIONAL DEBT MANAGEMENT

In the following an analysis of elements of banks' institutional framework relevant for decisions in international lending and asset trading is presented. The focus is on US institutions in particular, first, because of the dominance of US banks in this business, and, second, because of the relatively more restrictive effect of US regulations compared to regulations of other jurisdictions. For an exemplary comparison, the respective German institutions are considered as well.

The major part of this chapter concerns sector-specific regulations. The three categories that will be analyzed are supervisory and tax laws as well as accounting conventions. Because of their combined influence there is substantial interdependence between institutions of all categories[64]. Subsequently the most relevant firm-specific institutional determinants will beg presented. In addition to sector- and firm-specific determinants, also factors that originate in the political sphere impact rescheduling country debt management. Two of these will be considered here.

Bank supervision and taxation are important policy tools for the governments of banks' domicile countries for inducing a specific behavior for commercial banks. The actions of banks' home governments are primarily concerned with the domestic part of the international financial sector. By establishing a large number of different national regulatory regimes they provoke a multitude of strategic adaptations by banks to their respective institutional environment. This gives rise to international institutional arbitrage.

For example, together with supervisory laws and accounting requirements, especially tax laws have a significant impact on the risk treatment of banks as they determine a bank's policy towards building reserves. The treatment of risk as

64 Certainly, especially in cases of rescheduling country debt swap transactions also the sector-specific institutional framework in the respective debtor countries plays a significant role in individual banks' decision making. However, the scope of this study does not allow a treatment of these various countries' regulatory regimes (v. *Chamberlin/Gruson/Weltchek* [1988, 424seqq.]). For a survey of some rescheduling countries' debt equity swap regulations v. *Rubin* [1987] and *Wulfken* [1989, 164seqq.].

suggested by the results of an individual bank's country risk analysis can be distorted by the impact reserve increases have on cash flows and the distribution of dividends. Also the expected attitude of supervisory authorities - giving rise to the risk of regulatory change - is relevant in this context (cf. *Watson* et al. [1986, 66]).

4.1. SECTOR-SPECIFIC REGULATORY DETERMINANTS IN THE UNITED STATES OF AMERICA

The involvement of US banks in rescheduling country lending is demonstrated by table 7.

Table 7: US Banks' Claims on Selected Rescheduling Countries 1982-1988 (US$ millions as of end December each year)[a]

Country	1982	1984	1985	1986	1987	1988
Brazil	21955	24822	23572	23624	22270	20508
Mexico	24287	25783	24440	23545	22398	17567
Argentina	8576	8420	8736	9046	9230	7954
Venezuela	11223	10554	9787	8733	8056	7616
Chile	5887	6371	6249	6254	5871	4667
Philippines	5500	5126	5108	4930	4383	3629
Morocco	720	829	863	763	740	650
Nigeria	1725	1322	922	646	632	531
Costa Rica	452	434	421	399	317	214

----

[a] - Total exposure owed US banks after adjustments for guarantees and external borrowings.

Source: *FFIEC* [1989; 1988; 1987; 1986; 1985; 1983].

4.1.1. Supervisory Determinants

Supervision of commercial banking in the USA is organized in two tiers. Banks that choose to be chartered on a state level are supervised by the regulatory agencies of the individual states and concurrently with the Federal Reserve Board (FRB) if a bank has chosen to be a member of the Federal Reserve System. Banks that choose to be chartered on the national level are supervised by the Office of the Comptroller of the Currency (OCC) in the Treasury Department and are required to be members of the Federal Reserve System. In addition, national banks are and state banks may be required by their regulators to become members of the the Federal Deposit Insurance Corporation (FDIC). Since 1978 the Federal Financial Institutions Council (FFIEC) prescribes uniform principles and standards for the federal examination of banks by the respective agencies (cf. *AICPA* [1984, 1]).

A Joint Memorandum of the OCC, the FRB, and the FDIC of April 1983, which became law with passage of the Domestic Housing and International Recovery and Stability Act of 1983 (DHIRSA) recognized the transfer problems of many debtor countries and proposed to:

1. *Strengthen the existing program of country risk evaluation and examination, including stricter capital adequacy requirements for those banks having large concentrations of credit in particular countries;*

2. *Increase public disclosure of the country exposure of banks including more frequent and more timely availability of aggregate data and public disclosure by individual banks of all country exposure concentrations;*

3. *Formalize and make uniform a system for reserving against certain country exposures (discussed in more detail below);*

4. *Change and make uniform the way income is reported from international loan fees; and*

5. *Increase international cooperation among foreign banking regulators and provide for greater sharing of IMF information.*[65]

4.1.1.1. Reporting Requirements

All deposit insured commercial banks and bank holding companies need to present various reports to the federal regulatory agencies at regular intervals. The most important report is the Quarterly Report of Condition and Income ("Call Report"). Its disclosure requirements depend on the volume of a bank's assets. This report contains a balance sheet, an income statement and specific information on loan losses, reserves, changes in equity capital accounts and the distribution of maturities and types of items in major asset and liability accounts (*Goldberg/Haendel* [1987, 64]).

Supervision for international lending separate from domestic lending was initiated by the OCC after 1963. Since 1977 a semiannual Country Lending Survey requires banks with foreign offices to list all loans to foreign debtors by amount, country and type of borrower, to indicate the remaining maturity of the asset and to state

---

65 Cited from *Goldberg/Haendel* [1987, 68].

whether any guarantor exists. In addition, since 1978 the OCC, the FRB, and the FDIC evaluate and comment on a bank's international exposures. Of special interest to the regulators are the procedures and sources of information used in country risk analysis and how country lending limits are established and implemented (*Goldberg/Haendel* [1987, 63]).

After the onset of the debt crisis in 1982, new regulations were introduced with the International Lending Supervisison Act of 1983 (ILSA). The ILSA requires banks to submit the Country Lending Survey on a quarterly basis (*12 U.S.C.A. § 3906(a)*). If the total amount of loans to a particular country surpasses 1% of total assets, a bank has to publish detailed information on the size and status of such loans. For exposures over 0.75% of total assets less detailed information is stipulated (*Lissakers* [1984, 52]). Furthermore, since 1985 the FFIEC requires information on the maturity structure of international loans as well as on the amounts of trade-financing credits and claims of branches of foreign banks in the USA on creditors in their home countries (*Goldberg/Haendel* [1987, 63seq.]).

4.1.1.2. Capital Requirements

One of the principal reactions of banks to the debt crisis, besides reducing their overall rescheduling country exposure, has been to increase their capital. While US bank loans to less-industrialized countries have been curtailed by US$ 32.1 billion from US$ 139.7 billion in June 1982 to US$ 107.6 billion in December 1987, US bank capital has almost been been doubled by US$ 63 billion from US$ 66.2 billion to US$ 129.2 billion within the same period. These developments led to a decrease of the percentage of the amount of loans to less-industrialized countries to capital from 211% in June 1982 to 83% in December 1987. The nine largest money center banks saw a decline of this ratio from 323% to 139% in the respective period (*GAO* [1988, 16]). The size of bank capital is important because it is used as a measure for determining maximum lending capacity and serves as a criterion for assessing a bank's capital market rating.

So far, regulatory equity capital has included general and specific loan-loss reserves - in particular most reserves established for country risk - besides common stock, surplus, retained earnings, reserves for contingencies and other capital reserves. International risk-based capital guidelines to be implemented in the USA by the end of 1990 and of 1992 respectively will require banks to structure their equity capital in two tiers - called core capital (tier 1) and supplementary capital (tier 2) - on the basis of four specificly defined risk categories of assets[66]. Tier 1 capital will by year-end 1992 have to represent at least 50% of total capital. Both tiers of capital together may not amount to less than 8% of risk-weighted assets. For transition purposes by year-end 1990 the ratio of capital to risk-weighted assets must reach at least 7.25% for total capital and 3.625% for tier 1 capital[67].

A limited amount of the allowance for loan losses will be counted as part of supplementary capital. However, ATRRs[68] and specific reserves are not included. By year-end 1990, the total allowance for loan and lease losses has to be limited to 1.5% of a bank's risk-weighted assets and by year-end 1992, these general loan-loss reserves may not exceed 1.25% of risk-weighted assets when counted as part of capital. Additional reserves will still be required in order to fully cover potential losses.

The risk weights for each category of assets are set at 0%, 20%, 50%, and 100% for categories 1, 2, 3, and 4 respectively (*Federal Reserve Bulletin* [1989, 166]. The majority of assets included in a bank's loan portfolio are part of asset category 4, weighted at 100%. This comprises for instance - among others - long-term cross-border claims on non-OECD banks, all claims on foreign public sector bodies, claims on commercial firms owned by the public sector, and investments in stock of domestic and foreign corporations. The risk-weighted categories of assets discriminate against loans to borrowers in non-OECD countries. The capital guidelines based thereon reduce the incentive for banks to increase the allowance for possible loan losses because it will not be considered part of core capital and

---

66 For an account of the evolution of the new capital standard originally proposed by the Basle Committee on Banking Regulations and Supervisory Practices v. *Bardos* [1987]. The proposal itself is contained in *BIS* [1987].

67 Core capital consists only of common stock, cumulative perpetual preferred stock (for BHCs only), noncumulative perpetual preferred stock, paid-in surplus, retained earnings, and minority interest in equity accounts of consolidated subsidiaries. Supplementary capital includes allowance for loan and lease losses, perpetual preferred stock and related surplus, hybrid capital instruments and mandatory convertible debt securities, term subordinated debt and intermediate-term preferred stock, including related surplus. For a detailed description of the new capital guidelines v. *Federal Reserve Bulletin* [1989].

68 V. section 4.1.1.5.

because only a portion of general reserves will be counted as supplementary capital.

4.1.1.3. Lending Limits

The introduction of country lending limits under the ILSA or the DHIRSA was explicitly avoided. Reasons cited included country-specific differences, political pressures and the already high level of some commercial banks' claims on particular countries. However, state and federal laws restrict the maximum amount a bank can lend to one borrower to 15% of its capital (*12 U.S.C. § 84*).

In 1979 an interpretive ruling of the OCC stated that this restriction also applies to loans to foreign governments and their entities and that for this purpose loans to the central government should be combined with loans to government agencies and instrumentalities unless: "(1) the borrower has resources or revenue of its own sufficient to service its debt obligations (the "means" test), and (2) the loan is obtained for a purpose consistent with the borrower's general business (the "purpose" test) (*Goldberg/Haendel* [1987, 68]). On the basis of such definition, lending to sovereign borrowers was not restrained to one sovereign entity per country but rather allowed to apply the lending limit to separate entities including for instance government-owned corporations. This made it possible that single country exposures of individual US banks exceeded the limit by multiples (cf. *Ongman* [1985, 687seqq.]).

There is also a restriction on the maximum amount a bank can invest in the securities of any one borrower. This limit is set at 10% of a bank's capital and surplus (*12 USC § 24(7)* and *12 CFR Part 1*). The regulatory agencies, however, have in various instances interpreted these rules in a way allowing the infringement of these limits when required as a consequence of a restructuring (*OCC/FRB/FDIC* [1989a, 22]).

4.1.1.4. Loan Classification Requirements

In 1979 the three supervisory agencies have constituted the Interagency Country Exposure Review Committee (ICERC) for conducting country risk analyses[69].

[69] The report of a detailed examination of the work of the ICERC and the procedures it applies is contained in *GAO* [1988].

Each agency appoints three of the nine members of this body. Before each of its three meetings per year, agencies' staff members prepare analyses of selected countries. They also consult with commercial banks. The resulting classification of individual countries into seven categories can be influenced significantly by foreign policy considerations of the government of the USA (*Goldberg/Haendel* [1987, 65], cf. also *Stokes* [1985, 2138]). However, no formal link exists between the U.S. Department of State and the tasks of the ICERC.

The classification is intended to reflect the significance of economic, social and political problems for a country's debt service capacity. Individual countries are rated strong, moderately strong, weak, other transfer risk problems (OTRP), substandard, value impaired, and loss. In examining international lending exposures these categories serve for determining the extent of reporting on risk concentrations and the perceived necessity for reserving against particular country risks.

Detailed commentaries are stipulated for concentrations of claims to countries of the "weak" category if these claims exceed 5% of a bank's capital. Such commentaries are deemed necessary for "moderately strong" countries at a threshold of 10% and for "strong" countries at a threshold of 25% of capital (*Goldberg/Haendel* [1987, 65seq.]). These commentaries, however, have no binding character for bank management and thus have no direct restraining effect on country risk exposure (cf. *Ongman* [1985, 692]).

As a consequence of the DHIRSA, the rating scale for international loans was changed. The previously applicable remaining classifications of substandard, doubtful, and loss were replaced by a four-tier scale, complementing the strong, moderately strong, and weak categories: OTRP, substandard, value-impaired, and loss. The new classifications were introduced for better representation of the degrees of failure to adopt or comply with bank rescheduling agreements, IMF or suitable adjustment programs, as well as noncompliance with terms of its existing foreign debt.

OTRP is used when debtors (1) are not complying with foreign debt service obligations but have adopted economic adjustment measures as a remedy; (2) fulfill their obligations at present but future noncompliance seems imminent; or (3) have been classified previously as substandard, value-impaired, or loss but have resumed debt service on a sustained basis. Substandard is applied when a country does not comply with the terms of existing debt, does not enter into rescheduling negotiations, and does not adopt an economic adjustment program.

Value-impaired is used when more than one of the following conditions is met: (1) interest has not been paid for six months - also known as the "180-day rule"[70]; (2) IMF programs have not been complied with; (3) rescheduling terms have not been met for over one year; and (4) no definite prospects for an orderly restoration of debt service in the near future have been shown. The classification loss is chosen when a claim is deemed uncollectible and of so small value that its maintenance as a bankable asset is not warranted. A debtor's decision to repudiate its debt to bank creditors serves as a criterion for applying this rating (*Goldberg/Haendel* [1987, 65]).

4.1.1.5. Reserve Requirements

The supervisory authorities in the USA stipulate the building of "allowances for loan losses" for coverage of certain and anticipated loan losses (*12 CFR § 208.16* in conjunction with *17 CFR § 219.9-03 No. 7* and *§ 210.9-04 No. 11*). Both asset-specific and general reserves are included in the allowance (*Mendelowitz* [1987, 8])[71]. However, the level of allowances is not specified and may vary from bank to bank. After Regulation Y Art. 43 (*12 CFR § 225.43*) - until implementation of the risk-based capital standards - the allowance is counted as part of a bank's capital.

Therefore a bank's lending capacity is reduced when allowances are set off by loan losses. Thus, the main purpose of these regulations is to entice prudent lending behavior by requiring banks to increase the allowance in line with the perceived riskiness of loans extended. This reduces profits in the respective period. The decision on the establishment and size of these reserves rests exclusively with bank management, although the methods applied for determining the amount of reserves are examined by bank supervisors.

---

70 This rule has for instance been very influential in pushing US bankers to quickly convince bankers from other domicile countries to arrive at a quick approval to the 1987 Brazilian rescheduling (cf. *Williamson, M.L.* [1988, 20]).

71 The distinction between specific and general reserves refers to whether the reserve is allocated to a particular asset or not.

Table 8: Developing-Country Exposure and Loan-Loss Coverage of large U.S. Banks at Year-end 1987

Bank	DCE[a] in % of assets	DCE in % of primary Capital	DCE net of LLR[b] in % of sharehol-ders'equity	Developing country LLR-co-verage in %	Charge-off in 1987 (US$m.)
Citicorp	6.5	79	113	25	214
BankAmerica Corp.	10.8	124	245	20	234
Chase Manhattan	8.7	112	171	25	78
Manufacturers Hanover	12.1	145	263	22	63
J.P. Morgan & Co.	7.2	74	81	25	149
Chemical NY	7.6	97	151	25	21
Security Pacific	3.0	39	36	54	78
First Interstate	2.7	36	34	54	150
Bankers Trust NY	7.1	80	104	25	55
First Chicago	6.6	75	98	39	91

----

a - Developing-country exposure.
b - Loan-loss reserve.

Source: Salomon Brothers, *Review of Bank Performance*, 1988 Edition; cited after *Huizinga* [1989, 133].

In addition, the ILSA allows the federal regulatory agencies to require banks to set aside so-called "allocated transfer risk reserves" (ATRR) for international loan assets which are classified as "value-impaired" as a consequence of transfer problems of the debtor that prevent orderly debt service in the long run. A bank can choose to establish a reserve or to charge off the required percentage of the asset. The condition for such classification is that:

> *(A) the quality of such banking institution's assets has been impaired by a protracted inability of public or private borrowers in a foreign country to make payments on their external indebtedness as indicated by such factors, among others, as (i) a failure by such public or private borrowers to make full interest payments on external indebtedness; (ii) a failure to comply with the terms of any restructured indebtedness; or (iii) a failure by the foreign country to comply with any International Monetary Fund program or any other suitable adjustment program; or*
>
> *(B) no definitive prospects exist for the orderly restoration of the debt service (12 U.S.C.A. § 3904(a)(1)).*

ATRRs have to be charged against current income, shall not be considered as part of capital and are separated from the allowance for loan losses (*12 U.S.C.A. § 3904(a)(1)*). This in effect says that ATRRs reduce the scope for further new lending in the period in which they are established but do not reduce the lending capacity in case of actual losses. Hence, ATRRs better serve the provisioning requirements of banks.

However, despite this direction to establish ATRRs, the potential necessity of new lending for improving the liquidity of a troubled debtor country has been acknowledged. The amount and the timing for establishing ATRRs may differ from country to country and may also be dependent upon the type of the claim. The required percentage of the loan amount, however, is equal for all banks (*Goldberg/Haendel* [1987, 69]).

The size of the ATRR is determined at least once a year and is initially fixed at 10% of the loan amount. Further adjustments in future periods are added in ranges of 15%. As of June 1989, claims on 11 countries had been classified "value-impaired" and on 1 country "loss"[72], representing only 16% of total outstanding bank debt owed by less-industrialized countries (*NZZ* [30. Juni 1989, 13]). Information on which countries are classified "value-impaired" and at what percentage the respective ATRR has been set is confidential[73]. Banks are free to choose higher reserve levels.

ATRRs have so far not been required for debtors such as Brazil, Mexico, or Argentina. This and the fact that the restraining effect on exposure is reached only after a problem has arisen, i.e. after classification, makes ATRRs a rather ineffective instrument to constrain sovereign lending (cf. *Ongman* [1985, 701]). Foreign loans classified as "loss" have to be completely written off[74].

---

72 Interview of the author with officials at the Office of the Comptroller of the Currency.

73 However, it is not always treated confidentially. For example, as of July 1987 the ATRR has been set at 90% for Sudan, for Zaire at 75%, for Peru at 30%, and for Bolivia at 50% (*Baumann* [1987, 391seq.]). In June 1989 an ATRR of 20% was also required for Argentina (*FAZ* [13. Juni 1989, 23]).

74 For a survey of other countries' reserve requirements v. *Peat Marwick* [1986, 14].

Table 9: Reserve Rates Required by ICERC[a]

Classification	Debt owed US-American banks (US$ billion)	Required reserve rates (percent)
OTRP	37.9	0.0
Substandard	21.6	0.0
Value-impaired	11.2	32.7[b]
Loss	n.a.[c]	100.0
	total 70.7	average 7.4[d]

----

[a] - Book value of debt as of December 1988; required reserves up to June 1989; required reserve rates based on weighted average of book value.
[b] - Percentage calculated on the base of book value just prior to the setting of reserve requirements. Banks generally respond to reserve requirements by writing down assets by the required amounts causing a decline in book value.
[c] - Total exposure was less than US$ 0.1 billion, but not presented in order to prevent disclosure of confidential, individual country reserve requirements.
[d] - Based on exposure as of December 1988. The required reserve rate for "value impaired" loans does not use December 1988 exposure as a base.

Source: Debt Owed from FFIEC's Country Exposure Lending Survey, April 1989; required reserve rates from US federal bank regulators. Cited after *Mendelowitz* [1989, 11].

4.1.1.6. Accounting for Fees

A further regulation introduced with the ILSA stipulates that fees that are charged by banks for debt restructurings shall not exceed the actual cost for administrating this restructuring. Should a fee exceed this amount amortization over the effective life of the loan is required (*12 U.S.C.A. § 3905*). The previous practice was to record any fees for international lending as income in the period they were received. The introduction of this directive was motivated by law makers' perception that this provided an incentive for boosting earnings by engaging in reschedulings and extensions of new loans (*Ongman* [1985, 709]).

4.1.1.7. The Ninety-Day-Rule

Of significant influence on the debt management process has been the "ninety-day-rule". This rule which applies to domestic as well as international loans requires banks to classify as "non-performing" such loans for which interest payments are more than 90 days overdue. After this date any interest income accrued during this period has to be subtracted again, and any new interest due cannot any more be recorded as income in public financial statements. Such loans are consequently placed on a "non-accrual", i.e. cash basis which implies that income can only be recorded when it is received in cash (*Mendelowitz* [1987, 12])[75].

The significance of the effect of this rule cannot be underestimated as debtor countries have already successfully deferred rescheduling negotiations until this ninetieth day (*Guttentag/Herring* [1989, 35]). In case a bank places an asset on non-accrual, a loss has to be recognized immediately. If a provision is allocated to a particular loan, this may eliminate any interest income on that loan. Should this loan be on non-accrual status, provisioning uses up other income and weakens the bank's capital position (*Link* [1984, 77])[76].

In August 1988, a "Statement on Recording Interest Payments on Certain Sovereign Debt" was issued by the regulatory authorities. This statement established a guidance on when to record as income interest payments from a sovereign debtor that had interrupted regular debt service for a substantial period. However, it also did not provide a definitive formal guidance on when a debtor country could be returned to accrual status (cf. *Baumann/Harvey* [1989, 14]).

4.1.1.8. Debt Equity Swap Regulation

An impediment for banks wishing to conduct debt equity swaps has been Regulation K of the Federal Reserve Board. Until February 24, 1988, Regulation K prohibited banks to hold equity securities of nonfinancial companies abroad, exept such investment could be categorized as a "portfolio investment" (*12 C.F.R. § 211.5(d)(13)(1988)*)[77]. After issuance of proposed amendments in 1987 the FRB in

---

75 FFIEC, Reporting Form No. 031 ("Consolidated Reports of Conditions and Income"). The law, applicable to banks chartered in New York, provided for a 60 day period, but then was extended to 90 days to allow for parity of treatment between state and national banks in the face of the sovereign restructuring crisis. New York State Banking Law, § 109 (cited after *Link* [1984, 78, n. 7]).

76 For tax purposes, however, this rule does not apply. Thus, banks in this context continue to accrue interest income and are subject to tax on such accrued but unpaid income.

77 Cf. for a detailed discussion of Regulation K provisions and subsequent amendments concerning debt equity swaps *Rubinstein* [1988] and *Gruson* [1988]. V. also *Roth* [1989, 83seqq.] and *Wulfken* [1989, 210seqq.].

1988 revised Regulation K by introducing the final version of these amendments after having received comments from banks and law makers.

These new provisions allow bank holding companies - not individual banks - to convert sovereign debt of rescheduling countries for 100% equity interests only in government-owned companies that are to be privatized. For all other nonfinancial companies, debt equity swap investments are only allowed up to a share of 40% of the equity interest. If the interest exceeds 25%, it is required that another investor unrelated to the BHC owns a larger share of voting power. Supplementary loans and credits to the company may not exceed 50% of the total credit received. The bank's board representation in the company is to be proportional to its equity interest.

The investment has to be limited to a maximum of 15 years unless the government of the respective country allows a shorter holding period in which repatriation of capital and dividends is possible. In this case, Regulation K only allows this period plus two years as the maximum holding period. Finally, the general FRB consent limit for such investments is set at the lower of 1% of the BHC's equity capital or US$ 15 million. Notice of investments exceeding this treshold has to be furnished 45 days in advance of the transaction. The permission may, however, still be withheld by the FRB (*Rubinstein* [1988, 177]).

With a "no objection" letter the OCC, in November, 1987, exempted national banks from an obstructive rule contained in the BHCA *(12 U.S.C. § 1843(c)(2)(1982)*) to engage in debt equity swaps in satisfaction of debt previously contracted. Ownership in this case is limited to 60% of the equity interest (cf. *Gruson* [1988, 491seqq.] and *OCC/FRB/FDIC* [1989a, 19])78. An important condition for the application of this exemption is that a bank must conclude that swapping debt for equity ultimately places the bank in a better position than holding on to the respective sovereign debt.

---

78 Also, national banks, state chartered banks, Edge Corporations, and bank holding companies can accept to obtain equity interests in creditor companies in order to prevent a loss on such credits when a restructuring is necessary. This way of compensating concessions on debt by acquiring a claim on future earnings of the company - which does not represent a debt equity swap - has been applied in several cases, most notably to Mexican companies (*OCC/FRB/FDIC* [1989a, 18seq.]).

4.1.2. Tax-related Determinants

4.1.2.1. Reserves

The tax treatment of reserves for bad debts is the central tax-related determinant for an explanation of international lending behavior of banks. In the USA, the Tax Reform Act of 1986 (TRA) included the instruction that banks with assets of greater than US$ 500 million have to deduct loan loss provisions from profits after tax. Only smaller banks can continue to deduct additions to loan loss reserves from taxable income. However, these are generally not engaged in international lending.

Charge-offs, but not reserves, required by the regulatory authorities - such as ATRRs - as well as actual charge-offs of loans continue to be tax-deductible (*Baumann* [1987, 395 & 427]). Before the introduction of the TRA it was possible to deduct a maximum of .6% of eligible loans for additions to the bad debt reserve. Now, for determining the deductibility of bad debts only the "specific charge-off method" is used whereas previously the so-called "reserve method" could also be used. The specific charge-off method only allows to deduct such losses that are actually charged off.

As a consequence, US tax authorities only accept direct charge-offs of loans that are categorized as loss for deduction. Many US banks view this change as an obstacle for early write-offs of rescheduling country loans. They fear that the Internal Revenue Service (IRS) will put individual charge-offs under enhanced scrutiny and will require much more evidence of the worthlessness of the particular loan portion written-off.

For accepting a charge-off for deduction, worthlessness has to be determined by applying criteria established by the IRS (*26 U.S.C.A. § 166 (a)(1)*). This implies that the lender has to prove beyond reasonable doubt that the respective asset is truly uncollectible (*Mendelowitz* [1987, 16seq.]). Mere doubts about the collectibility of the loan are not sufficient to give rise to the assumption of worthlessness. Given a reasonable expectation of a restoration of debt service, a loan cannot be considered worthless.

Voluntary charge-offs are considered deductible by the IRS only when presented with a certification of loan worthlessness by bank regulatory agencies. Banks supervised by the Federal Reserve are able to obtain such certifications and are therefore at an advantage compared to banks supervised by the OCC and the FDIC, which do not receive certifications of charge-offs.

The criteria of worthlessness had not been designed for international loans but for domestic purposes only and are therefore of limited applicability to assessing country risks. For example, the IRS rules stipulate that the creditor must have taken all reasonable steps to collect the claim. Before assuming worthlessness, also any possible legal action should have been taken. Another rule would make it difficult for one bank to justify any charge-off of a loan to a particular borrower unless all other creditors of the same loan did not do the same. Tax deductibility for an individual bank in this case would depend upon charge-offs undertaken collectively by all creditors (*Mendelowitz* [1987, 17seq.]).

4.1.2.2. Debt Reduction Modes

In addition, there remains significant ambiguity as to the fair valuation of asset exchange transactions for tax purposes[79]. Tax consequences differ depending on the characterization of the associated commercial relationships of an exchange transaction. After Revenue Ruling 87-124, the IRS follows an interpretation that in selling a loan with a discount the bank incurs a loss in the amount of the discount.

In case of a direct conversion of debt into an equity investment the loss for the bank is measured by the excess of its tax basis in the loan - the principal amount - and the fair market value of the local currency received in the exchange. In transactions involving charitable organizations like in case of debt for nature swaps the bank is considered to incur a loss determined as in a direct conversion and is granted a charitable contribution deduction equal to the fair market value of the amount of local currency received. In the fair market valuation of the amount of local currency received all facts and circumstances of the exchange have to be taken into account. If such valuation cannot be arrived at with reasonable accuracy it is assumed that such value equals the value of the property surrendered - the

---

[79] For a description of the relevant issues in determining the "adequate" tax treatment of sovereign loans subject to reschedulings and/or exchange transactions v. *Baumann/Harvey* [1989, 14seq.].

value of the principal amount of the loan minus the discount (*Chamberlin/Gruson/Weltchek* [1988, 461]).

4.1.2.3. Foreign Tax Credit Determination

On April 28, 1989 the IRS with Notice 89-58 - effective for taxable years beginning after December 31, 1986 - reduced the foreign tax credit advantages accruing from the allocation of loan losses stemming from rescheduling country loan charge-offs. US corporations are taxed on the basis of worldwide income. Any US corporation with subsidiaries or branches in foreign countries may either deduct taxes paid on income from such foreign sources as expenses or may credit these foreign income taxes against US income tax. The latter route is mostly more beneficial. However, there exists a maximum amount for the applicable foreign tax credit. It must not exceed the amount of foreign tax paid or accrued and is subject to the following income limitation:

$$MFTC = \frac{FSTI}{WTI} \times USITBC$$

Where:

MFTC - maximum foreign tax credit
FSTI - foreign-source taxable income
WTI - worldwide taxable income
USITBC - US income tax before the credit

Unused parts of the credit that result from this limitation can be carried back two years and forward five. The calculation of MFTC is applied separately to each of a number of "baskets" (classes) of income (*Touche Ross* [1989, 491seq]). With passage of the TRA, profits on the sale of certain foreign assets were reclassified as domestic income (*IRC § 865*). Implicit in this new rule was that losses resulting from such sales would also be treated as domestic. Thus, US banks counted losses from sales of rescheduling country loans that represented foreign assets as domestic losses which did not reduce foreign income. This, in turn, allowed maximum use of foreign tax credits (cf. *Saunders* [1989] and *Baumann/Harvey* [1989, 16]).

However, with issuance of IRS notice 89-58[80] on April 28, 1989 losses on foreign loan sales by US banks are now required to be counted as foreign according to the relative size of a bank's international lending business as compared to its entire

---

[80] Sec. 5 of IRS notice 89-58 contains the guidance in question:

A loss derived by a bank from the disposition, or specific charge-off under section 166 of the Code, of an eligible loan shall be allocated to the class of gross interest income derived by the bank from its portfolio of eligible loans. Where such interest income includes both U.S. and foreign source income, or foreign source income includable within more than one separate limitation category under section 904(d)(1), such loss must be apportioned between or among these residual and statutory groupings. The apportionment shall be made according to the tax book value asset method as described in section 1.861-9T(g) of the regulations (relating to the apportionment of interest expense), subject to the following rules:

(a) In applying the asset apportionment method, the average value of eligible loans held by a bank shall be treated as its only assets. Accordingly, losses realized with respect to eligible loans will be apportioned among the statutory and residual groupings based on the proportion of the average value of eligible loans giving rise to income in such groupings.

(b) The average value of eligible loans outstanding within each statutory or residual grouping will be determined by utilizing the beginning of the year and end of the year averaging method described in section 1.861-9T(g)(2) of the regulations. The average value of eligible loans, however, shall not be computed utilizing the fair market value method of apportionment.

(c) The transition rules contained in section 1012(h)(7) of the Technical Corrections and Miscellaneous Revenue Act of 1988, Pub. L. No. 100-647, related to allocation and apportionment of interest expense are not applicable for purposes of this notice.

(d) Any loan that qualifies as an exempt asset as defined in section 1.861-8T(d)(2)(ii)(A) of the regulations shall not be treated as an eligible loan as defined in section 4, paragraph (c) of this notice.

(e) Eligible loans attributable to a foreign branch of a domestic corporation shall be taken into account as assets in a manner that is consistent with section 1.861-9T(f)(2) of the regulations, and losses on such loans shall be included in the amount of losses subject to allocation and apportionment under this notice.

(f) A loan to a related person within the meaning of section 267(b) shall not be treated as an eligible loan.

(g) In the case of an affiliated group that is eligible to file, but does not file, a consolidated return, allocation and apportionment of losses on eligible loans will be subject to adjustments similar to those described in section 1.861-11T(g) of the regulations.

lending business. Hence, in case a bank's foreign business represents 40% of its total business and its domestic business represents 60%, then 60% of the foreign losses would count as domestic and 40% as foreign. On the other hand, the same apportionment also applies to losses on domestic loans which therefore partially count as foreign.

The effectiveness and rationale of this rule rests on the potential future introduction of an even more stringent rule that would require banks to allow deductions of all foreign loan losses only against foreign income and domestic loan losses only against domestic income (*Saunders* [1989]). This would make it more beneficial for banks with a large international exposure to engage in writing off some of their rescheduling country loans under the regime of notice 89-58 than under a potentially more detrimental future rule. This measure therefore can be conducive to the promulgated stipulations of the Brady-Plan[81].

4.1.2.4. Charitable Contributions

A rule intended to provide incentives to spur the use of swaps involving charitable contributions such as mainly debt for nature swaps is Revenue Ruling 87-124. Previously, tax deductions for charitable contributions were limited to the market value of a loan when such value was below the tax basis of such loan. In case the lender wanted to donate the debt, only the market value, and not the cost basis, i.e. the face value, would be considered for tax deduction. Whereas in case the lender would have sold the loan in the secondary market and donated the proceeds to charity it would be entitled to tax deductions both on the loss it incurred, i.e. cost basis minus market price, and on the donation.

Therefore, in order to facilitate direct charitable contributions and to even out the income effects of both routes, Revenue Ruling 87-124, issued in November 1987, allows banks to deduct donations to charitable organizations specified in section 501(c)(3) of the IRC equal to the cost basis of the underlying asset. An additional benefit could lie in the fact that the amount of redemption of debt obtained by a

---

81 Apart from these bank-specific rules, also debt equity swap investors have to consider tax implications pertinent to the evaluation and decision on whether to engage in a debt equity swap or not. The IRS Advance Revenue Ruling 87-124, IRB No. 1987-14 addresses some questions that arise with a debt equity swap transaction (v. *Faria/Stott/Buchanan* [1988]).

US conservation agency in rescheduling country local currency could be higher than the price attainable in a secondary market transaction. The valuation of the local currency received in exchange for the debt is to be based on the free market exchange rate of the local currency in order to apportion the deduction between the loss incurred in the exchange and the charitable contribution (cf. *Hyde* [1988] and *Oberndörfer* [1989, 22]).

4.1.3. Accounting Determinants

Accounting rules consist of legal and non-legal regulations. Generally, laws specify accounting requirements and rules issued by professional organizations lay down how these requirements are to be implementeted. Although the latter are based on laws, they are agreed-upon behavioral principles only of a quasi-legal character.

Accounting of US banks' international lending activities is guided by Generally Accepted Accounting Principles (GAAP) as well as by the instructions contained in statements of the Financial Accounting Standards Board (FASB) and the rules contained in the Council of the American Institute of Certified Public Accountants' (AICPA) "Audit of Banks". In addition, the Securities and Exchange Commission (SEC) issues accounting guidelines to be adhered to by publicly traded companies concerning issues not adressed by the FASB. These are contained in staff accounting bulletins (SABs), in Article 9 of Regulation S-X, and the related Industry Guide 3.

The relevant accounting rules for loan losses and the treatment of loan swap and rescheduling transactions are contained in: (1) Statement of Financial Accounting Standards No. 5, "Accounting for Contingencies" (SFAS No. 5), (2) Statement of Financial Accounting Standards No. 15, "Accounting by Debtors and Creditors for Troubled Debt Restructurings" (SFAS No. 15), (3) Staff Accounting Bulletin No. 75 "Accounting and Disclosure by Bank Holding Companies for a 'Mexican Debt Exchange' Transaction" (SAB No. 75), (4) AICPA's Practice Bulletin No. 4 "Accounting for Foreign Debt/Equity Swaps" ,and (5) that part of the AICPA Industry Audit Guide: "Audits of Banks", which refers to the classification scheme established by the regulatory authorities for reserves and loans subject to country risk (cf. *Baumann* [1987, 422] and *OCC/FRB/FDIC* [1989a, 4]).

4.1.3.1. Reserves

The AICPA prescribes the following guidelines for the establishment of an allowance for loan losses:

> *A bank should maintain a reasonable allowance for loan losses applicable to all categories of loans through periodic charges to operating expenses. The amount of the provision can be considered reasonable when the allowance for loan losses, including the current provision, is considered by management to be adequate to cover estimated losses inherent in the loan portfolio (AICPA [1984, 61seq.]).*

According to the AICPA reserves are defined as follows:

> *Legal reserves and reserves for contingencies. Such reserves are considered appropriated (restricted) retained earnings. The term "reserves" has been used to represent either valuations against asset accounts or liabilities; but, these reserves should be classified as valuation allowances or liabilities, as appropriate (AICPA [1984, 197]).*

Table 10: Standard Income-Statement Format

1. Interest Income
2. *Less:* Interest Expense
3. *Less:* Provision for Loan Losses
4. *Plus:* Noninterest Income
5. *Plus:* Gains (Losses) on Securities Not Held in Trading Accounts
6. *Less*: Noninterest Expense
7. *Less:* Applicable Income Taxes
8. *Plus:* Extraordinary Items and Other Adjustments Net of Income Taxes
9. *Equals:* Net Income (Loss)
10. *Less:* Dividends Declared
11. *Equals:* Addition to (Subtraction from) Retained Earnings

Source: *Guttentag/Herring* [1989, 6].

SFAS No. 5 stipulates to charge a loan-loss "provision" (item 3 in table 10) to income in the income statement when it is probable that a loss of loan principal has occurred the amount of which can be reasonably estimated. In this case an "allowance" or "reserve" (items 2 and 15 in table XX) in the same amount has to be established on the balance sheet as a negative entry on the assets side. The entirety of all such entries has to be sufficient to cover all losses inherent in a bank's loan portfolio (*FASB-Current Text* [1987, C59.128seq., C59.105, V18]). It is not permitted to use existing capital or retained earnings to build up the allowance (cf. *Mendelowitz* [1987, 8]). Should the amount of the provision exceed the amount of net income during one period, the excess amount is deducted from retained earnings (item 17 in table 11)[82].

When a certain amount of loan principal is deemed uncollectible a "charge-off" (item 13 in table 11) is made directly against the allowance and the respective loan account is reduced by the same amount. The opposite procedure applies in case of unanticipated recoveries (item 12 in table 11). GAAP require that charge-offs and reserves have to be recognized in the period of this determination of uncollectibility. They cannot be spread over more than one period as this would impair the credibility of financial statements. In case of actual loan losses it might be necessary to restore the allowance anew to a desired level through charges to income. Substantial fluctuations of profits as a consequence of loan losses can thus be avoided by a prudent reserve policy (*Mendelowitz* [1987, 8seq.]).

---

82 This is what happened in the second quarter of 1987 when many US banks increased their loan loss reserves to an unprecedented size. Citibank added a LDC loan-loss provision of US$3 billion to a US$403 million provision for losses on its remaining assets - totalling US$3.403 billion. This amount exceeded its quaterly income by US$2.585 billion - the highest quarterly loss ever reported by a US commercial bank. After addition of declared dividends of US$117 million retained earnings (items 9 and 20 in table 11) were reduced by US$2.702 billion (*Guttentag/Herring* [1989, 5seq.]).

Table 11: Standard Balance-Sheet Format

Assets
1. Assets
2. *Less:* Loan-Loss Reserve
3. *Equals:* Net Assets

Liabilities
4. Deposits
5. *Plus:* Other Liabilities
6. *Equals:* Total Liabilities

Equity Capital
7. Common and Perpetual Preferred Stock
8. *Plus:* Capital Surplus
9. *Plus:* Retained Earnings
10. *Equals:* Total Equity Capital
 Net Assets (3) - Total Liabilities (6) = Total Equity Capital

Memorandum item: Loan-Loss Reserve
11. Loan-Loss Reserve Balance at End of Previous Reporting Period
12. *Plus:* Recoveries
13. *Less:* Charge-Offs
14. *Plus:* Provision for Loan Losses (item 3 in Table 10)
15. *Equals:* Loan-Loss Reserve (2)

Memorandum item: Retained Earnings
16. Retained Earnings at End of Previous Reporting Period
17. *Plus:* Net Income (item 9 from Table 10)
18. *Less:* Cash Dividends Declared (item 10 from Table 10)
19. *Plus:* Foreign-Currency Translation
20. *Equals:* Retained Earnings (9)

Source: *Guttentag/Herring* [1989, 7].

4.1.3.2. "Troubled Debt Restructurings"

SFAS No. 15 has to be applied by creditors and debtors involved in loan restructurings. This statement determines the disclosure requirements applicable to "troubled debt restructurings". A troubled debt restructuring is one in which assets, other than cash, or equity interest are transferred from the debtor to the creditor instead of contractually agreed payments or in which the terms of the debt are modified like through extending maturity dates or changing interest rates. If the total expected cash payments from a particular loan after a rescheduling are less than the remaining balance of existing claims the resulting difference has to be written off. If the expected payments under the modified terms are equal or greater than the remaining balance no loss is deemed to have occurred; no writedown is required (*FASB-Current Text* [1987, D22, 11825]).

This rule leads to the use of longer repayment periods, as it becomes less likely that writedowns are required as a consequence of concessions the longer this period is chosen. Therefore the opinion is prevailing that SFAS No. 15 allows banks not to recognize loan losses. On the other hand, GAAP require that SFAS No. 15 is used in conjunction with SFAS No. 5 which determines whether a specific claim is uncollectible. Hence, whenever a restructured claim is deemed uncollectible, charges to income have to be made in order to reflect the economic loss that has occurred. In practice, the determination of uncollectibility is a very subjective matter that may differ from bank to bank (*Mendelowitz* [1987, 9seq.])[83].

Most reschedulings of less industrialized country debt, however, have not been characterized as troubled debt restructurings. Thus, no loss needs to be recorded under SFAS No. 15 in connection with these restructurings, because the future cash receipts, both principal and interest, are still deemed sufficient to recover the recorded investment (*Baumann* [1987, 391] and *Schroeder/Swegle* [1987, 59]). Interest rates charged for new loans were considered to represent market rates.

In case of such qualification SFAS No. 15 stipulates certain disclosures. The SEC has directed attention to the problems involved in deciding whether a troubled debt restructuring can be assumed and has issued its own disclosure requirements. These requirements encompass even more information than does SFAS No. 15.

Therefore, banks with publicly traded stock have to follow the SEC rules and have to disclose in their annual reports the total amount of loans to a particular country disaggregated for the private, public, and banking sector and for maturity if this amount exceeds 1% of total assets or 20% of primary capital. Total country exposures that are greater than .75% of total assets or 15% of primary capital have to be reported only in aggregate (*Grabbe* [1986, 243]). In addition, disclosure of potential problem loans as of the current year, loan concentrations over 10% of the current portfolio, the total amount of claims restructured, old and new interest

---

83 For an analysis of the valuation principles relevant for an interpretation of SFAS No. 15 which are contained in the Statement of Financial Accounting Concepts (SFAC) No. 5 v. *Holzmann* [1989].

rates, the effect on income, and all other changes involved in the rescheduling is required.

4.1.3.3. Secondary Market Transactions

Whereas these rules do not prevent banks from reserving against or writing down rescheduling country debt, the accounting treatment of swaps of such debt involves two barriers for better diversification of US banks' loan portfolios. Such swaps are required to be valued at current fair value. Whereas GAAP require loans made by the bank expected to be held until maturity in its loan portfolio to be recorded at cost, i.e. principal amount less an amount reflecting permanent diminution in value, loans that are traded are to be held at the lower of cost or market in its separate trading portfolio (cf. *Chamberlin/Gruson/Weltchek* [1988, 465]).

An AICPA "Notice to Practitioners on Foreign Loan Swaps", issued in May 1985, established a guidance which characterizes a swap of loans to different debtors as an exchange transaction involving monetary assets. As it is assumed that the earnings process associated with the particular loan is completed at the date of the transaction, current fair value is the measure for valuation. If the current fair value of the loan received is greater or less than the debt given, a gain or loss has to be recorded at the time of the transaction.

In the notice it was assumed that generally the current fair value of debt received will be lower than the value of the debt given, which would result in recording a loss. This means that if a bank enters into a par swap, i.e. the face values of the respective debts equal each other, the bank has to recognize a loss although this transaction might not affect the overall value of its loan portfolio. However, it was acknowledged that the determination of current fair value is a highly subjective and difficult procedure, particularly as the secondary market is viewed to be underdeveloped. Therefore, in the valuation process, other indicators such as loan sales (for cash), prevailing market interest rates, underlying credit risk, and similar debt instruments should also be considered (*Mendelowitz* [1987, 14seq.]).

A second problem arises with the fear that in case two debts are swapped and a writedown of the debt swapped is required, banks in the future will be forced to mark to market, i.e. to write down the debt principal of all remaining comparable claims to current fair value - a measure known as "tainting" or "portfolio contamination". Current practice does not require such marking to market of the remaining claims as long as any loss recognized in the swap transaction is not related to ultimate collectibility, and bank management has not shown any intention to dispose of the remaining claim before maturity (cf. *Baumann/Harvey* [1989, 5]).

Especially larger US banks fear that with further increase and standardization of secondary market transactions auditors may require marking to market. Such a change would result in severe reductions of reported earnings (*Mendelowitz* [1987, 15]). This also explains the frequent public announcements by banks that the recording of provisions for loan losses does not imply an impairment of face value. Accountants differ in their opinions on how to treat this problem. One party favours the application of historical cost accounting principles which would permit to carry debt of various values simultaneously. A change in this fundamental accounting principle is not foreseen. Another party holds the view that if secondary market activity increases substantially, marking to market is the only reasonable procedure for valuation (*Mendelowitz* [1987, 16]).

4.1.3.4. Debt Equity Swaps

Rules concerning the accounting for debt equity swaps are not unequivocal and may therefore have varying effects on bank earnings. One possible procedure has been outlined by *Baumann* [1987, 424seq.]. If debt equity swaps are characterized as exchange transactions, as it is currently done by the AICPA with PB No. 4, valuation of such transactions should be based on their current fair value. Then a problem arises with determining what exactly current fair value is. Traditionally, both the fair value of the assets given and the assets received are considered for valuation. This approach is especially relevant if the value of the assets given is not readily determinable, or does not accurately indicate the value of the assets received.

AICPA's PB No. 4, released in 1987, suggests the following indicators to establish fair value: (1) Similar transactions for cash, (2) estimated cash flows from the equity investment or net assets received, (3) market value, if any, of similar investments, and (4) currency restrictions, if any, affecting dividends, the investment's sale, or the repatriation of capital (cf. *Baumann/Harvey* [1989, 5])[84]. Then, a potential indicator for the determination of fair value could be the prices negotiated in the secondary market for rescheduling country debt.

However, the Chairman of the Board of Governors of the Federal Reserve characterized these prices as "*not reliable indicators of underlying value*"[85]. A similar opinion has been voiced by the Deputy Comptroller of the Currency[86]. This is why auditors do not consider the use of only the secondary market price an appropriate basis for valuation[87].

As a consequence, also the fair value of the equity interest received needs to be determined. Both valuations then can be used for an appraisal of the fair value of the transaction which is in line with GAAP[88]. Besides clarifying that debt equity swaps should be regarded as exchange transactions for accounting purposes, PB No. 4 provided US banks with an additional incentive to enter into debt equity

---

84 *Holzmann* [1989, 13seqq.] explores the derivation of the guidelines of AICPA's PB No. 4 from the conceptual accounting principles of relevance and reliability laid down in SFAC No. 5.

85 Letter of the Chairman of the Board of Governors of the Federal Reserve, Paul A. Volcker to U.S. Senator Bill Bradley from November 6, 1986 accompanying a report on the secondary market prepared by the Federal Reserve, cited here after *Baumann* [1987, 425].

86 "*...Applying the term "secondary market" for LDC loans can be very misleading and confuse important related issues, such as asset valuation and accounting treatment. The term "secondary market" conjures images of depth, breadth, volume, rate and yield structures, homogeneous instruments-borrowers-terms-rates-legal underpinnings, and primary market makers. Little of this infrastructure is found in the LDC debt market. Therefore, the prices quoted reflect the high level of operating imperfections present. In my view the "secondary market" is a bazaar and not an institutionalized arrangement which should be used as the proxy for valuing assets totalling over $400 billion. These circumstances, and my views, may change but for now, I believe we want to be very careful about using the term "secondary market" as it applies to LDC loans.*" (*Bench* [1987, 10]).

87 The same problem exists for German banks in determining the tax deductibility of loan loss provisions.

88 For the accounting aspects to be considered in the valuation of swap transactions involving debt equity conversion funds v. *Baumann/Harvey* [1989, 6seq.].

swaps for their own account as the associated book loss could turn out to be less than the secondary market discount.

Losses on debt equity swaps are to be charged against the allowance for loan losses. A bank could even be able to recover a loss or record a gain in case the respective loan had previously been bought in the secondary market or had already been partially written down. However, after PB No. 4 such loss recoveries or gains ordinarily should not be recorded until the equity investment or net assets received in the exchange are realized and repatriated in US dollars (cf. *Chamberlin/Gruson/Weltchek* [1988, 467]).

4.1.3.5. Debt for Debt Swaps

Securitization of loans through swaps for bonds is accounted for differently according to whether the bank treats the bond as a loan or as a security. If the bond is intended to be held until maturity it can be carried as a loan being valued at amortized historical cost less loan write-offs and loan loss allowance. Any loan losses will flow through the loan loss allowance. If it is intended to be sold, it is carried in the investment securities portfolio at the lower of amortized historical cost less any loan write-offs or fair value (*Hanley et al.* [1989, 1])[89].

The accounting treatment of exit bonds is usually governed by SFAS No. 15, as was the case with the exit bond element of the 1988 Brazilian refinancing program (*OCC/FRB/FDIC* [1989a, 13]). However, the 1988 Mexican debt swap transaction involving the tendering of US$ denominated loans to Mexican public sector entities for US$ denominated bonds, of which the principal has been collateralized by zero coupon US Treasury securities, had been interpreted as an exchange transaction and not as a troubled debt restructuring. Hence, fair value accounting was required. Application of SAB No. 75 consequently resulted in a respective write-down or allowance according to the tender price. Similar adjustments of the remaining claims not tendered are not required under SAB No. 75. It only asks for

---

89 Accompanying the 1988 Mexican debt for bond swap offer a letter from the auditing firm Price Waterhouse & Co. to all potentially participating banks voiced the opinion that this transaction was to be treated as an exchange of monetary assets and accounted for at fair value (cf. *Chamberlin/Gruson/Weltchek* [1988, n. 131seqq.]).

continued screening of the remaining Mexican and other rescheduling country loan portfolio as to the adequacy of allowances (*Baumann/Harvey* [1989, 7]).

In the case of the Mexican debt for bond swap of 1990 the SEC has ruled that both the reduced principal and the reduced interest bonds offered in the exchange can be accounted for at book value even if the market value of the bonds is lower. However, this is only possible as long as the total undiscounted amount of cash flow to be earned over the lifetime of the bond exceeds the face value of the old loan. It was stated that such debt swaps should be treated as modifications of existing loan agreements (*World Bank* [1989b, 28]).

4.1.3.6. Debt for Nature Swaps

Different from debt equity swaps, in a debt for nature swap no recovery of dollar assets is anticipated. Thus valuation in this case depends on the amount of local currency or bonds or property or services involved in the exchange (*U.S. Accounting: A Summary* [1988])[90].

In sum, the classification of debt transactions as either troubled debt restructurings or exchange transactions is the central accounting question of relevance for a bank manager's decision on entering into such transaction. Classification as an exchange would require immediate loss recognition and valuation at the cost or market value. In case of an exchange for cash the market price indicates the value. In case of an exchange against other assets the fair value is to be established by taking into consideration other factors, such as particularly the value of the asset received.

---

90 In the case of an Ecuadorian debt for nature swap marketable government bonds in local currency equal to the full face value of the foreign currency debt - based on the official exchange rate - have been issued. These bonds are managed by a foundation in order to provide a steady income stream for supporting the protection and expansion of parks, buffer zone activities, and environmental education (*"U.S. Accounting: A Summary"* [1988]).

4.2. SECTOR-SPECIFIC REGULATORY DETERMINANTS IN THE FEDERAL REPUBLIC OF GERMANY

In order to demonstrate the difference of national sector-specific regulations and their impact on bank behavior the relevant German institutions are considered in the following. Germany is another important domicile country of banks involved in less-industrialized country lending. The involvement of German banks in lending to selected rescheduling countries is illustrated by table 12.

4.2.1. Supervisory Determinants

Banking supervision in the Federal Republic of Germany is carried out by the Bundesaufsichtsamt für das Kreditwesen (BAK) and the Deutsche Bundesbank. Until 1980 no regulatory provisions existed that took explicit account of country risk. The Banking Act (Kreditwesengesetz - KWG) had been designed for a domestic domain only. The existence of a risk category separate from the individual risk of non-payment that arises as a consequence of country-specific factors was taken up as a regulatory issue for the first time on January 18, 1980 in a letter of the BAK to the Institut der Wirtschaftsprüfer (Institute of Auditors). In this letter, the BAK points out that the responsibility to avoid high exposures to country risks rests exclusively with the management of the individual bank.

4.2.1.1. Reporting Requirements

With this letter, the requirement was introduced that auditor's reports must contain information on the methods applied to country risk analysis, and their effects on loan portfolio management and the determination of lending limits. By decreeing the Länderrisikoverordnung of December 19, 1985, the BAK required banks to disclose more detailed information on their country risk exposure in a "Meldung zum Auslandskreditvolumen gemäß § 25 Abs. 4 KWG". Banks that hold loans to foreign debtors with a total amount in excess of DM 100 million must report to the Deutsche Bundesbank the total amount of all such claims to all debtors per country, the amount of collateral security (such as guarantees, letters of awareness etc.), and the total amount of loan loss provisions (Einzelwertberichtigungen and Rückstellungen) recorded for these loans if the total amount of such claims exceeds DM 1 million per country.

Table 12: German Banks' (domestic domicile, foreign branches, and foreign subsidiaries of German banks) Claims on Selected Rescheduling Countries (DM millions as of end December each year, 1989 end March)

Country	1984	1985	1986	1987	1988	1989
Brazil - total	**15268**	**15012**	**14084**	**13560**	**13716**	**14631**
German domicile	6221	7236	7618	7579	8188	8575
foreign branches	2319	2019	1728	1683	1695	2027
foreign subsidiaries	6728	5757	4738	4298	3833	4029
Mexico - total	**11065**	**9397**	**7586**	**6556**	**6632**	**6791**
German domicile	1688	2140	1942	1887	2375	2427
foreign branches	4894	3887	3015	2413	2553	2644
foreign subsidiaries	4483	3370	2629	2256	1704	1720
Argentina - total	**7635**	**7522**	**7147**	**7079**	**8396**	**8053**
German domicile	2019	3065	3228	3511	4053	3875
foreign branches	1918	1682	1470	1312	1811	1553
foreign subsidiaries	3698	2775	2449	2256	2532	2625
Venezuela - total	**6067**	**5210**	**4121**	**3565**	**4126**	**4375**
German domicile	1578	1511	1402	1331	1497	1527
foreign branches	1957	1547	1111	920	951	1082
foreign subsidiaries	2532	2152	1608	1314	1678	1766
Philippines - total	**1489**	**1359**	**1187**	**902**	**841**	**923**
German domicile	357	362	419	496	492	488
foreign branches	507	471	410	159	115	130
foreign subsidiaries	625	526	358	247	234	305
Nigeria - total	**4506**	**3895**	**3464**	**2851**	**2267**	**2216**
German domicile	3408	3114	2808	2164	1616	1575
foreign branches[a]	-	-	-	-	-	-
foreign subsidiaries	1098	781	656	687	651	641
Poland - total	**7272**	**7590**	**7273**	**6864**	**6662**	**6575**
German domicile	4997	5126	4819	4509	4720	4679
foreign branches[a]	-	-	-	-	-	-
foreign subsidiaries	2275	2464	2454	2355	1942	1896
Costa Rica - total	**168**	**189**	**160**	**121**	**121**	**124**
German domicile[a]	-	-	-	-	-	-
foreign branches	168	189	160	121	121	124
foreign subsidiaries[a]	-	-	-	-	-	-
Egypt - total	**2965**	**3338**	**3513**	**3651**	**3790**	**3852**
German domicile	2933	3322	3483	3633	3769	3838
foreign branches	32	16	30	18	21	14
foreign subsidiaries[a]	-	-	-	-	-	-

----

[a] - Not available or insignificant.

Source: *Deutsche Bundesbank* [1989, 52seqq.].

4.2.1.2. Reserve Requirements

There are no regulatory provisions for German banks geared to international lending only. Basically, there are three categories of loan loss reserves that banks can establish: Einzelwertberichtigungen, Sammelwertberichtigungen, and Globalwertberichtigungen as allowed by § 26 (a) KWG. Einzelwertberichtigungen (specific reserves) are designed to be applied to individual loans. As country risk is regarded as specific risk, specific reserves are appropriate.

However, as country risk applies to all loans to borrowers in a particular country irrespective of the individual loan, banks usually create a global loan loss allowance for these discernable risks (Pauschalwertberichtigung). These are established as a sum of the respective individual loan loss provision as long as there are no other individual provisions due to a separable risk of non-payment of a particular loan or as long as there exists no collateral for such claims (*Luckey* [1987, 291]). On the basis of § 40 HGB in conjunction with § 155 AktG, banks are free to determine the amount of such global provisions themselves. Except through informal statements, conversations with bank managers, and unofficial references to average provisioning levels at other banks, the BAK does not intervene in this valuation process.

Until end-1988, another category of provisions has been the so-called "vorgeschriebene Sammelwertberichtigung" (prescribed general reserve). Banks have been required to record Sammelwertberichtigungen for certain assets. They are general loan loss provisions for undiscernable risks, i.e. they serve to protect a bank's capital against latent but non-specifiable risks. In this case, the BAK stipulated minimum levels to be established at every bank. For example, loans with a maturity in excess of four years which are not secured by any lien on landed property, had to be provided for with 0.5% of their book value. However, on August 18, 1988, the BAK issued an order which abolished this provisioning vehicle (cf. *Stannigel* [1989, 260]).

§ 26 a KWG in conjunction with § 253 (1) and (3) and § 279 (1) Satz 1 HGB gives banks that are corporations (Kapitalgesellschaften) the right to use a lower valuation standard than § 253 (1) and (3) HGB would demand as long as with "reasonable commercial judgement" (vernünftiger kaufmännischer Beurteilung) this is deemed necessary for the protection against the particular risks of the banking business. § 253 (1) and (3) HGB requires to value assets either at historical cost (Anschaffungskosten) or at a lower value derived from a market price or otherwise established with "reasonable commercial judgement"[91]. This way, by establishing so-called Globalwertberichtigungen, banks can create hidden reserves in order to avoid large fluctuations of earnings in financial statements. They are not tax-deductible.

An additional instrument for creating a cushion for capital protection that can be applied to international loans are Rückstellungen. Rückstellungen are provisions for unspecified expenses which are relevant for the respective reporting period but not exactly quantifiable because of pending actions. Thus, they also include imminent losses from pending commitments. Rückstellungen are treated as liabilities. Their creation reduces profits. One case for which Rückstellungen have to be created is the furnishing of a guarantee for a subsidiary that would otherwise have to record a negative net income as a consequence of a need to acknowledge provisions for loan losses.

Except for the now abolished decree on minimum levels for Sammelwertberichtigungen, no supervisory rules specify criteria for determining the amount of provisions for loan losses. With § 26 a KWG, the regulators have explicitly approved of a possibility to create hidden reserves with German banks. Other ways to build up hidden reserves are the dexterous application of generally accepted accounting principles or the adoption of permissible valuation options like the non-recognition of an increase of an asset's value after previous recording of write-offs (cf. *Epperlein* [1987, 145]).

The extent to which events like a declaration of a moratorium, a rescheduling agreement, or debt service irregularities serve as criteria for assessing an adequate level of provisions, is entirely left to the discretion of senior bank management. However, on the basis of § 26 Abs. 1 and § 44 Abs. 1 KWG, the BAK is entitled to

---

91 In addition, § 254 HGB also allows to write down a loan from book value to a newly established value, if this new value is in line with tax law prescriptions.

receive any information on a particular bank's business in addition to that provided through its financial statements and auditor's report if it wishes to do so.

Table 13: Indicative Country Risk Reserve Levels with German Banks

Country	Percentage Write-Downs
Argentina	40-80
Bolivia	50-100
Brazil	45-75
Chile	40-70
Cuba	80
Iraq	20-40
Iran	20-40
Mexico	40-70
Nigeria	30-60
Peru	60-100
Philippines[a]	10-40
Poland	50-100
Romania	25-60
South Africa	25-40
Yugoslavia	35-60

a - Data from 1985-1986.

Source: *World Bank* [1989a, 86] and *Faria/Stott/Buchanan* [1988].

4.2.1.3. Capital Requirements

According to the criteria applied to define equity capital - fully paid in, available to absorb current losses, and available long-term - principally only common stock and paid-in surplus (offene Rücklagen) have so far been accepted to constitute bank capital in Germany. Details are specified in § 10 KWG. General loan loss reserves have not been considered as part of capital. However, until 1992 German bank capital requirements will be altered in order to conform with the capital guidelines formulated by the Commission of the European Comunity which again are based on the international risk-based capital guidelines issued by the Basle Committee on Banking Regulations and Supervisory Practices[92]. Otherwise, because of the narrower definition of capital applied in Germany today, German banks would be in a competitive disadvantage, especially because of the leverage effect of capital for business volume.

92 V. section 4.1.1.2. and *Berger* [1989].

4.2.1.4. Lending Limits

Regulations relevant for a bank's risk management are the Grundsatz I of the BAK in conjunction with § 10 KWG, § 13 and § 13 a KWG, and § 14 KWG. Grundsatz I requires that the total amount of all loans and equity interests minus all provisions created for such assets and deferred liability items shall be less than eightteenfold the amount of capital. § 13 and § 13 a KWG stipulate that all loans exeeding in amount 15% of capital, i.e. so-called Großkredite, have to be announced to the Deutsche Bundesbank immediately, the total amount of all such Großkredite shall be less than eightfold the amount of capital, and the amount of an individual Großkredit must not exceed 50% of capital. § 14 KWG requires banks to report to the Deutsche Bundesbank the debtors of loans that exceed DM 1 million in amount.

4.2.1.5. Debt Equity Swap Regulation

The KWG also imposes restrictions as to banks' ability to invest in nonfinancial companies - as for instance by means of debt equity swaps. § 12 Abs. 1 and Abs. 2 Ziff. 1 KWG stipulates that the total book value of all investments in land and buildings, plant and equipment, ships, shares in credit institutions, claims resulting from silent partners' equity interests and from profit participation certificates, and equity interests in financial and nonfinancial companies are not to exceed a bank's liable equity capital. However, if the equity interest in a nonfinancial company does not exceed 10% of its stock capital, this restriction does not apply. Furthermore, § 24 Abs. 1 Ziff. 3 KWG requires immediate notification of the BAK and the Deutsche Bundesbank in case of any such investment in other companies.

4.2.2. Tax-related Determinants

Global loan loss provisions for discernable risks - Pauschalwertberichtigungen - have so far generally been accepted for tax deduction by the tax authorities. It is important to note, however, that there may be delays of up to six years until the tax authorities have accepted or rejected a particular reserve level (cf. *World Bank* [1989a, 81]). For such acceptance, the valuation criteria applied have to be derived from objectively verifiable ("*objektiv nachprüfbar*") circumstances[93]. Therefore, the tax authorities have to ascertain a valuation standard for determining tax deductibility. So far, they have not taken any final decision as to what standard will be applicable to loans to rescheduling countries. Neither secondary market prices, nor country risk-rating schemes, nor any internally developed assessment procedure have been accepted[94].

Faria/Stott/Buchanan [1988] point out that practice between 1982 and 1985 indicates that reserve levels up to 40% or 50% are acceptable for most rescheduling country debtors. As in Germany tax returns are based on commercial accounts, German banks record high provisions in their commercial financial statements in order to claim recognition of relatively high amounts of loan loss provisions by the tax authorities (cf. *ibid.*).

Sammelwertberichtigungen have been tax deductible as long as they had been created for loans falling into the category of loans for which minimum levels of these provisions are required (v.s.). Loans to sovereign debtors, other public sector borrowers and banks as well as loans guaranteed by the aforementioned or otherwise indemnified, however, did not fall into this category and were therefore implicitly deemed to be risk-free by the BAK[95]. These general provisions for undiscernable risks have been tax deductible up to the minimum level stipulated as long as they were created for the assets specified.

Prior to the abolishment of the duty to create Sammelwertberichtigungen, on July 4, 1988, German tax authorities withdrew the recognition of tax deductability for such provisions. However, banks may choose to apportion the tax effects of the dissolution of Sammelwertberichtigungen over the years until 1990 by establishing a "Sonderposten mit Rücklageanteil", i.e. a deferred tax liability item. This

93 BFH v. 3.7.1962, BFHE Bd. 124, 343 and BFH v. 13.3.1964, BFHE Bd. 79, 529. An important decision for this context was the decision by the fiscal court of the state of Hessen of September 16, 1983 in which a provision in the amount of 50% of face value and 100% of unpaid interest of a loan extended to a Polish bank by the German subsidiary of a US bank can be accepted by the authorities (*Betriebsberater* [1984, 36]).

94 Based on an interview with a representative of the Bundesamt der Finanzen.

95 Cf. Anordnung über die Bildung von Sammelwertberichtigungen bei Kreditinstituten, vom 17. September 1974 (BAnz. Nr. 180 v. 26.9.1974).

deferred item may amount to two thirds of the amount dissolved but has to be recognized in the income statement per 50% in 1989 and 1990 (*Stannigel* [1989, 260seqq.])[96]. Global provisions after § 26 a KWG (Globalwertberichtigungen) are not tax deductible.

4.2.3. Accounting Determinants

Generally, the accounting provisions of §§ 238-335 of the German Commercial Code (Handelsgesetzbuch - HGB) are also applicable to banks. Specific accounting rules for banks are laid down in §§ 25a-26b KWG. As already stated, for loan valuation banks have to follow § 253 (1) and (2) HGB, which stipulates to use historical cost unless a market price can be identified. In addition, if a market price cannot be identified and a lower valuation than historical cost is deemed reasonable, this value is to be used. Swaps of loans for other assets would generally be accounted for at fair value of that asset, loan swaps at market or fair value. Debt equity swaps would also be recorded at the fair value of the investment. Should such fair value be difficult to establish, the market value of the debt exchanged could normally be used (*World Bank* [1989a, 84]).

Loan loss reserves are recorded as follows: Einzelwertberichtigungen (specific reserves) are usually subtracted directly from the respective assets and are not recorded as a liability (*Birck/Meyer* [1977, II 327seq.]). The size of these specific provisions can be determined exclusively by bank management. The same applies to global allowances for discernable risks (Pauschalwertberichtigungen). Sammelwertberichtigungen can both be disclosed either as a negative item on the assets side or on the liabilities side. Rückstellungen have to be recorded on the liabilities side. Global provisions (Globalwertberichtigungen) after § 26 a KWG can be deducted from the respective assets. By using the cross-compensation method (Überkreuzkompensation)[97], banks are offered an opportunity to create long-term hidden reserves (*Arndt* [1986, 177]). They are not publicly disclosed but reported to the BAK.

---

96 The Sonderposten mit Rücklageanteil from this dissolution of Sammelwertberichtigungen on the balance of the largest German bank, Deutsche Bank, comprised DM 159 million (*Deutsche Bank* [1989]).

97 Cross-compensation means the netting of expenses incurred from provisions with extraordinary income from the dissolution of provisions.

4.3. COMPARISON

The following table 14 summarizes some essential features of the regulatory frameworks for German and US banks. A direct comparison of the beforementioned institutional conditions for international lending by US and German banks is made difficult by the incongruities of nomenclature and structural set-up of corresponding institutions. Whereas the German regulatory system is centralized and applies a rather informal approach to controlling banks, the US system - being much more decentralized - employs a more stringent regime (cf. *Dale* [1984, 97]). Another relevant factor for an understanding of the differences lies in the relatively stronger focus on short-term considerations in the USA[98]. For instance, German banks face less stock market pressures than US banks (cf. *Faria/Stott/Buchanan* [1988]). In addition, there remain substantial uncertainties on some tax and accounting questions. However, some major consequences of differences can be pinpointed as follows:

(a) US institutions are significantly more transparent and detailed as to disclosure requirements and valuation standards for tax and accounting purposes. This may be one reason why US banks are more reluctant to create provisions that reduce net income - given that the primary evaluation instrument for investors are its financial statements[99]. A high level of loan-loss provisions may be perceived as a signal for an impairment of creditworthiness. In other words, bank managers in the USA perceive higher participation costs arising from reporting than bank managers in Germany (cf. *Guttentag/Herring* [1989, 21]).

---

98 Whereas the SEC requires publicly held corporations to report financial statement data on a quarterly basis, there are no legal reporting regulations in Germany covering periods of less than a year.

99 Key indicators of credit quality for bank security analysts are the ratio of loan-loss provisions to net charge-offs and the ratio of loan-loss reserves to total loans (*Guttentag/Herring* [1989, 9]).

Table 14: Comparison of Supervisory, Tax and Accounting Institutions in the USA and Germany

	USA	Germany
Reporting Requirements		
Hidden Reserves	**no**	**no**
Foreign Loans	**yes**[a]	**no**
Amount of Non-Performing Loans	**yes**[b]	**no**
Reserve Policies		
Reserves for LDC Loans	**general (rarely specific)**	**specific**
Required Level of Reserves for LDC Loans	**varies**[c]	**industry average**[d]
Reserves Included in Primary Capital	**yes**	**no**
Tax Deductibility of Reserves		
Specific Reserves	**100% if classified "value-impaired"**	**up to 50% of reserves**
General Reserves	**minimal**	**minimal**
Loan Losses	**100%**	**100%**
Bank's Average Reserve Level for LDC Loans	**22%**	**52%**

a - Large US banks must disclose foreign assets by broad categories, and provide more detailed information on country exposures that exceed 0.75% of the bank's assets or 10% of total foreign exposure.
b - US banks must also disclose the amount of interest not accrued when a loan falls into arrears of more than 90 days.
c - Reserves required only for loans to countries classified as "value-impaired", that are at least six months overdue on interest payments to banks.
d - Bank supervisors require banks to maintain reserves at close to the national bank average for each debtor.

Source: *Williamson, M.L.* [1988, tables 3, 4, and 5].

(b) Because of this more liberal approach, German institutions, especially tax rules, have a far less restraining effect on earnings and therefore offer banks substantially more leeway and discretion for their provisioning policy. In fact, for US banks these differences represent a relative competitive disadvantage. They are bearing costs, namely a portion of those arising from provisions for loan losses, which banks in Germany can temporarily transfer to tax payers. This represents an implicit subsidy for German banks and at the same time provides an incentive to accept relatively higher risk exposures. In light of this incongruity the more generous US tax rules before the TRA had been more compatible with international standards.

(c) As German banks have more freedom in establishing a valuation standard for reporting purposes over the long run, they are able to build hidden reserves more easily than US banks and are therefore less vulnerable to sudden needs for provisions or writedowns. US banks have to create reserves or writedowns out of current earnings whereas German banks can simply use existing hidden reserves.

(d) Whereas German banks have to establish reserves for new loans in the same amount as for existing exposure, US banks need not necessarily allow for potential loan losses. In fact, they are at a comparative disadvantage as to their inability to deduct such provisions from taxes. On the other hand, institutions such as the ninety- and 180-day rules force US banks into new lending in order to assure regular debt service and, thus, to avoid substantial cuts in income. This regulatory policy is certainly not in line with the prudential objectives of banking regulation (cf. also *Williamson, M.L.* [1988, 17]). It also prevents interest capitalization instead of fresh money lending for US banks because capitalized interest might be treated as taxable income. In Germany, however, the possibility of pretax deduction of capitalized interest from accrued income would entice German banks to use this transaction mode.

(e) Through mandating the establishment of ATRRs - which requires a respective charge-off - the US supervisors can influence a bank's willingness to engage in future new lending, thereby directing banks to financially support such countries that abide by the performance criteria established with passage of the ILSA.

(f) As reporting requirements in the USA are much more extensive than in Germany the impact of accounting rules on lending and asset trading decisions is more relevant for US than for German banks (cf. *Williamson, M.L.* [1988, 17]).

(g) Differences in institutional conditions lead to a different readiness of creditors for participating in debt reschedulings. Especially concerning fresh money commitments, the constraining effects of Grundsatz I and the eventual necessity to record loan loss provisions for new loans to the same extent as for old loans to the same borrower, together with the possibility to capitalize outstanding interest into principal make German banks more reluctant than US banks. For US banks the ninety day-rule is a significant behavioral determinant as it has compelled them to keep borrowers liquid by extending new loans in addition to rescheduling old ones.

(h) Tax deductibility of reserves leads to contrary effects on US and German banks' willingness to participate in debt reduction transactions. Some German banks would have to record a taxable gain as their level of specific reserves is relatively high. In this case they would forgo an interest-free tax credit which is a consequence of the pretax deductibility of provisions. Also, remaining assets would have to be revalued which would raise the taxable gain further (cf. *World Bank* [1989a, 83seq.]).

(i) The avoidance of the application of SFAS No. 15 has been a major reason why US banks have taken the position to refinance debtor country obligations rather than granting concessions for principal and interest.

(j) As to possibilities to engage in direct debt equity swaps, the ambiguous US institutional framework clearly prevents US banks from more active participation in direct conversions of their claims for this purpose. On the other hand, also German banks are restricted in this respect. As to the selling of debt to non-bank investors wishing to engage in debt equity swaps, however, the above-mentioned arguments concerning secondary market transactions apply.

This divergence of institutional conditions for conducting rescheduling country debt transactions is an important reason also for differing business strategies of banks in this business and therefore complicates concerted efforts to induce fresh money lending by commercial banks. Table 15 provides an overview of the relevant conditions also in Canada, France, Japan, Switzerland and the United Kingdom. It is the function of the so-called menu approach to achieve such concerted ("case-by-case bank-by-bank") action despite these institutional obfuscations.

Table 15: Comparison of Regulations on Commercial Bank Provisioning against Rescheduling Countries in Selected Industrial Countries at End-1987

Country	Level of provisioning[a]	Mandatory provisioning	Tax deductibility of provisioning	Gearability[b]
Canada	30-40	Yes; 30-40% against basket of 34 countries	Yes	No
France	30-40	No[c]	Yes; but for provisioning in excess of average provisions on a case-by case basis	Yes
Germany	30-70	No[d]	Yes; but case-by-case	No
Japan	5	Yes; 1-5% for 36 countries	Yes; but limited to 1% of rescheduled debt and increased exposure	Partly[e]
Switzerland	30-50	Yes; 30% against a group of countries	Yes; but for provisioning in excess of mandatory proision on a case-by-case basis	No
United Kingdom	25-35	Bank of England guideline:	Yes; 80% of the provisioning value derived from Bank of England matrix 5-100% depending on country	No
USA	25-60[f]	No[g]	No[g]	Yes

----

[a] - In percentage of relevant exposure; numbers indicate ranges for major banks.
[b] - Indicates whether provisions are included in the capital base used to monitor capital-asset ratios.
[c] - Provisioning suggested against a number of countries with payment difficulties.
[d] - Adequacy judged against a number of countries with payment difficulties.
[e] - Only the non-tax-deductable portion is included.
[f] - Some regional U.S. banks have substantially higher provisions.
[g] - Except when loans are determined to be "value-impaired".

Source: IMF data. Cited after *Huizinga* [1989, 139].

4.4. FIRM-SPECIFIC DETERMINANTS

The previously presented sector-specific behavioral determinants have to be incorporated into the evaluation and decision-making processes that are institutionalized inside a bank as part of a bank's general strategy and organization and, more specifically, financial policy. The most important issues in this respect are considered now.

4.4.1. Strategy and Organisation

From a strategic perspective, the most important background consideration for deciding on engaging in secondary market operations is the planned scope of international involvement relative to the total business. A high degree of involvement in international business generally implies relative information cost advantages. Greater familiarity with business conditions in particular countries should enable such banks to better assess country risks but also to gain a share of the local market. Banks with an extensive network of branches and subsidiaries in many debtor countries may not perceive a need to dispose of their claims because it could hurt the future development of their local businesses.

On the other hand, involvement in the secondary market offers cross-selling opportunities, for instance with customers interested in debt equity swap transactions. Another strategic aspect are established relations with certain governments or with clients that have business interests in particular countries. If a particular bank takes a leading role in rescheduling negotiations, it can also benefit from the relations thus established with leading representatives of the debtor country that in the long run may prove advantageous for future business transactions (*Wellons* [1985, 146]).

The degree of involvement in secondary market operations is partially dependent upon bank-specific organizational conditions. Since 1985, all major US bank holding companies and some smaller investment banks, also from the U.K., have instituted specialized asset trading units. Thus, for many banks the trading of rescheduling country assets has emerged as a self-sustaining part of their total business. This centralization of decisions on secondary market activities in one department allows a faster reaction to transaction offers and enables a more thorough involvement in the market in general. Previously, the execution of one transaction would have required a time-consuming coordination process between various departments.

Services rendered by such a department may include the consulting of investors on business opportunities in rescheduling countries, particularly associated with debt equity swaps (cf. *Ebenroth* [1988, 26]), the consulting of debtor countries on ways for debt reduction, f.i. through debt for bond swaps, and on avenues to attract foreign direct investment. They may also include rescheduling country loan portfolio management for other banks that shun the costs of setting up a separate rescheduling country merchant banking unit.

However, to be present in this market, also non-US banks would have to set up such a unit in New York and to be present in other financial centers like London, Zürich, Frankfurt, and Paris. Almost all Japanese and European banks have so far shunned this costly step[100]. Competence in the specifications of the underlying rescheduling agreements, tax, accounting, and supervisory ramifications is required.

An important determinant for an individual bank manager's decisions for international lending and asset trading transactions are the incentive schemes applicable for loan officers or traders. Incentive schemes are firm-specific institutions that support particular organizational designs. Salaries, especially at US banks, often contain performance-related elements based on quantitative volume or return characteristics of transactions which tend to favor short-term over long-term considerations of transactions.

An added feature of personnel management policies - particularly observable in US banks - has been the inexperience and mobility of international loan officers as witnessed by *Gwynne* [1983][101]. Such personnel policies can also be institutionalized by means of an incentive system. These may favor the reward of a loan officer who fulfills or surpasses assigned loan quotas but can not provide for negative sanctions should any future problems arise from the transactions he/she has carried out because of a move to a different post inside or outside the respective organization (cf. *Darity/Horn* [1988, 90]).

4.4.2. Financial Policy

The importance of financial policy as a determinant for the design of transaction modes in international lending is evidenced by the standard policy in financial management not to extend funds on a long-term fixed interest rate basis when

---

100 The only German bank active in the secondary market is the Westdeutsche Landesbank (cf. *Ebenroth* [1988, 26]).

101 *"I am far from alone ..."*. *Gwynne* [1983, 23].

refinancing depends on short-term Eurodollar deposits. This policy has led to the predominant use of the roll-over principle in Eurodollar lending to less-industrialized countries in the 1960s and 1970s. Thereby commercial banks were able to transfer a substantial part of the interest rate risk to the borrower and thus effectively reduced contractual preparation costs, but may also have induced higher enforcement costs.

Such principles are the elements of the bank-specific set of behavioral rules applied in financial management. The institutionalization not only of certain objectives but also of the methods and criteria for the evaluation and implementation of policies to reach these objectives are the basis for planning and decision-making processes in firms. This concerns particularly the intended level of objective attainment and the subsequent adaptions of these levels (cf. *Herrhausen* [1971, 355]). That part of this set of methods and criteria most relevant for this context is applied in what can be called rescheduling country portfolio management.

The valuation of loans and inherent risks, as for instance in country risk analysis, is the mainstay for a prudential financial policy. As has been shown above, supervisory law, tax law, and accounting regulations pose powerful outside restraints on evaluation and decision-making within an individual bank. On the other side, every bank sets its own internal standards as e.g. to the adequate amount of reserves or the relative importance of different indicators of creditworthiness.

The restraining effect of external institutions on financial policy is exemplified by the fact that US banks with heavy exposure to particular rescheduling countries are in fact prohibited from participation in the secondary market because of the magnitude of potential losses that would result from a revaluation of this exposure after conducting a trade in such debt. This result is expected as it has been left unclear by the AICPA whether in case of the swap of a loan to a particular country the entire remaining portion of exposure to this country has to be marked to market (cf. *Schwarz* [1987, 86])[102]. Most of these banks have therefore established

---

102 The ratio of the amount of exposure to the 15 Baker plan debtor countries to capital of the nine largest US banks stood at 197% at end-1982 and at 121% at end-1986 (*Morgan Guaranty* [1987, 3]).

a separate trading portfolio that allows to enter into secondary market transactions whenever opportunities arise. This trading portfolio only comprises loans that have previously been purchased on the secondary market. Claims of their own can only be transferred into this trading portfolio by conducting a face-value swap.

However, through mutual adaption bank-external institutions not only restrain bank-internal institutions but at the same time also offer opportunities for establishing rules that improve objective attainment. For example, in the case of a loan sale in the secondary market costs arise with the write-off associated with the discount on its face value. In order to avoid a loss, sufficient reserves have to be built up in previous periods. In the case of provisions, banks under German supervision can build up provisions that are tax-deductible which in effect represents an interest-free loan by the tax authorities that matures upon realization of the anticipated loss[103]. If provisions exceed the anticipated loss, an extraordinary gain is recorded. Thus, to the extent possible, such institutional influences give rise to regulatory, and in particular tax arbitrage by banks which may emerge as a decision-criterion in the management of the rescheduling country portfolio. Within the scope of the US-German comparison of regulatory institutions US banks are then given an incentive to shift loans onto the books of their German subsidiaries (cf. *Ebenroth* [1984, 911]).

Cornell/Shapiro [1986] have shown that changes in regulatory influence on banks' international lending decisions can also significantly affect banks' stock market valuation. This in turn finally represents another determinant for the behavior of a bank (cf. *Darity/Horn* [1988, 91seqq.] and *Bruner/Simms* [1987]). The design of bank-internal institutions therefore also will have to account for stock market participants' reactions[104].

---

103 Building reserves denominated in DM creates the additional problem of adjusting the hedging policy for the US$/DM exchange rate risk inherent in US$ claims.

104 A very good case example of this mutual feedback between stock market and bank-internal valuation is the Citicorp rescheduling country provisioning decision of May 19, 1987. V. *Guttentag/Herring* [1989, 27seqq.].

4.5. INTERNATIONAL POLITICAL DETERMINANTS

For purposes of completeness, in the following two exemplary aspects of the political sphere that impact the design of innovations in financial relationships with rescheduling countries, one originating in banks' domicile countries and one originating in the debtor countries, are presented. Both play a role not so much for the specific set-up of a particular financial instrument, but rather form part of the background for their emergence.

4.5.1. Foreign Policy Considerations

The USA being closely involved in the debt crisis, not only by virtue of the exposure of its commercial banks, but also geostrategically, particularly in the case of Mexico, has a strong interest in alleviating some of the economic circumstances of the debt crisis. The "Baker Plan" and the "Brady Plan"[105] both included stipulations that indirectly further foreign policy and economic interests of the USA and other industrialized countries. These plans originated in the administration of the respective US government and included promulgations addressed to commercial banks. However, banks were reluctant to go along with it (cf. *Wall Street Journal* [March 27, 1986]).

There is clear evidence (cf. *Darity/Horn* [1988, 51seqq.], *Cohen* [1986], *Sampson* [1982, passim] and *Gisselquist* [1981, 142passim]) that also without publicly known concerted political actions, foreign policy considerations often played a significant part in private bank lending decisions to less-industrialized countries[106]. Economic incentives such as explicit guarantees of the banks' domicile countries primarily serve the aim of export promotion but can also serve pure foreign policy objectives (*Kreile* [1987, 188seq.]).

---

105 Cf. sections 3.1.2. and 3.1.3.

106 V. also *Spindler* [1984, 205passim]. Another case in point are the lending relationships between West German banks and the East German government (cf. *Legg* [1985]). The only attempt to test the extent to which this conjecture can be matched statistically known to the author has been *Jain/Nigh* [1989]. Using event study data these authors found empirical support for such influence.

Whenever strategic interests of banks' domicile countries are affected by banks' lending decisons, the conjecture of the existence of an implicit guarantee, i.e. a tacit promise of support, is apparent. The bank's domicile country would then also be supposed to support the debtor country in case of serious economic troubles (*Kahler* [1986, 20]). Finally, from the fact that the domicile country governments carry the responsibility for the stability of the financial system it can be derived that an implicit insurance against default exists at least for the large money center banks (cf. *Kreile* [1987, 194]).

Against this background it is understandable that a substantial "part" of country risk may be located rather in the domicile countries of banks than in the borrowing countries themselves. This also surfaces in the opposite view that borrowing countries have some kind of taxing power over banks' home governments on the basis of political sympathy and even geographical proximity as f.i. in the cases of Mexico and the United States or Poland and Germany. They thus depend on those governments' continued willingness to provide transfer payments for future debt service (*Agmon/Dietrich* [1983, 492seqq.]). Under this interpretation country risk appears at least partially as a systemic phenomenon as the transferring country weighs the benefits of transfers to a variety of countries against each other. The traditional approach of country risk analysis suggests that such interlinkages do not exist.

4.5.2. Debtor Country Sovereignty Violation

"Economic subjugation and the foreign debt are the modern forms of what military blockades were in the past. The debt ... has become a modern expression of imperialism" (*Falcoff* [1986]). This viewpoint of the former Peruvian President Alan Garcia has not been shared in its radicality by most other debtor countries. On the other hand, eleven Latin American countries, the "Cartagena Group", repeatedly expressed their cooperative attitude (*Witcher* [1985])[107]. With the debt crisis extending into a political dimension because of the magnitude of possible

---

107 V. also the Declaration of Quito of January 13, 1984, issued by the Permanent Secretariat of the Latin American Economic Conference, which stresses the rejection of all forms of discriminatory or coercive economic measures for political reasons in resolving the economic crisis of Latin American countries. Contained in *Eskridge* [1985, 267seqq.].

defaults and the associated high degree of cross-national interdependence, however, the debtor countries use their political bargaining power to press for concessional terms on existing debt and further increases of new lending. In fear of the expectedly high costs of potential exclusion from international financial markets, radical unilateral measures such as Peru's debt service limitation on its then US$ 14.3 billion external debt to 10% of its total export revenues have been very rare so far (cf. *Pine* [1986])[108].

However, the above quotation points to the central political consequence of the debt crisis and international economic relationships in general from the perspective of debtor countries - the perception of the violation of sovereignty. A perceived loss of sovereignty has also become a concern for the USA because of an increase of foreign direct investment (cf. *Morgan Guaranty* [1989, 7seq.]). The argument of too high a degree of foreign influence has often been used against the granting of further investment incentives, e.g. in connection with debt equity swap programs, or to avoid "too much" interference by the IMF or even bank creditors in the management of the economy.

Any behavioral condition for the borrowing country applied to the extension of new money or a rescheduling requires - if implemented - a change of economic or monetary policy. This is clearly an interference in domestic political affairs although it may be accepted by this country. The negative tenor of the argument is better comprehensible if one speaks of the fear of sovereignty violation.

The significance of the idea of sovereignty violation as an argument in the domestic political debate depends very much on the acceptance of the particular economic, monetary and social policies of a government by the population[109]. There exists no absolute hostility against foreign influence. Such fear of foreign influence will be articulated only after a certain threshold of perceived

---

108 The formation of a debtor country cartel has not been considered so far either. *Kugler* [1987] investigated this issue and concludes that the necessary domestic political support in individual countries had been lacking.

109 The domestic political pressure fueled by this argument can eventually lead to moratoria as in the case of Brazil in 1987 and hence can be used by debtor governments as a threat in debt negotiations (cf. *FAZ* [6. Dezember 1986]).

interference is reached. This threshold again is dependent on the perception of specific economic and political advantages accruing from foreign influences.

In order to serve as a political argument, the violation of sovereignty needs to be perceived as a negative influence by a large number of the electorate. The mass media are usually the channel for the stimulation of such opinions. Discomfort as a result of personal contact with foreigners or foreign products may also occur; it may, however, be much less significant. The institutionalization of a perception of national identity or cultural cohesion, i.e. of a degree of patriotism, is an important condition for the applicability of such arguments. The more extensively this institution is applied, i.e. the greater the number of situations in which it plays a role in partially determining the behavior of people, the greater the inclination to perceive foreign influences.

This perception of belonging to a nationally or culturally separable group can be divided into three components (*Tajfel* [1982, 70]): 1. A cognitive component determines the knowledge of the belonging, 2. an evaluative component determines the subjective evaluation of the belonging, and 3. an emotional component determines the - varying - degree of the perception of the cognitive and the evaluative components. The relative weight of these components also has an impact on the inclination to fear foreign influence. Used in the political process, media influence both the emotional and the evaluative component.

It can be observed that sovereignty violation is feared to a greater extent in less-industrialized countries than in industrialized countries because of a perceived necessity or desire for higher welfare. Hence, low material living standards in less-industrialized countries are ground for industrial countries to stipulate for the implementation of measures intended to stimulate trade, lending, foreign direct investment, and technology transfer, and, thus increase the international economic competitiveness of less-industrialized countries.

The degree of economic interdependence with foreign economic actors is one determinant of both economic and political dependence. Especially the resulting political dependence gives rise to the potential use of the fear of foreign influence as a domestic political argument. Thus, the respective dominant interest groups of a particular country might deliberately use the perception of belonging to a national or cultural group (as a status quo) for specific domestic political objectives by stimulating the emotional or evaluative component of the perception of belonging. As long as the political and economic consequences of the fear of sovereignty violation are considered relevant by creditor banks and their domicile country governments, they have to take account of this phenomenon in the design of financial relationships.

5. EFFICIENCY ANALYSIS OF INNOVATIONS IN INTERNATIONAL DEBT MANAGEMENT

The following efficiency analysis focuses primarily on the relationship of creditor banks and rescheduling countries. Benefits or costs for other parties are alluded to only when their role directly impacts the explanation of the efficiency of a particular innovation as is the case for multinational corporations participating in debt equity swaps. All efficiency improvements perceived by creditor banks can also be considered as applicable criteria for their rescheduling country portfolio management decisions. Certainly, a host of positive and negative externalities for other parties exists that for matters of scope and simplicity cannot be discussed here.

5.1. SECONDARY MARKET TRANSACTIONS

As has been stated in section 2.4., the reduction of transaction risks implies a reduction of expected enforcement costs. However, in order to stress the effect of secondary market tansactions on expectations of costs, the reduction of transaction risks will first be considered separately. Then, the reduction of transaction costs will be treated in more detail.

5.1.1. Reduction of Transaction Risks

Rescheduling country asset trading in the secondary market has led to a variety of efficiency improvements from individual banks' perspectives. The principal effect of this medium has been the hitherto difficult spreading of risks associated with rescheduling country assets. The most substantial benefit in this case has been the responsiveness of trading mechanisms to the particular requirements of individual banks. Besides currency and interest rate risks, again the most relevant risk category is the country-specific risk of non-payment[110].

---

[110] Cf. section 2.4.1.

Asset trading allows the ex post diversification of rescheduling country loan risks by pooling a large number of different claims of various categories, maturities, currencies and on various countries. Thus, most perceived benefits that usually go along with securitization also apply to rescheduling country secondary market trading[111]. In addition, if the secondary market is used for reducing rescheduling country exposure, asset trading allows to make previously tied up risk bearing capacity available for other less risky loans. In this case, the relative amount of equity capital available to absorb losses from rescheduling country loans is increased[112].

In contrast to the trading of securitized claims, however, the transfer mechanisms for rescheduling country loans and the necessary consideration of a multitude of interdependencies with the underlying contractual relationships, asset trading still represents a relatively fussy process. This is reflected in the liquidity of this market which is increasing but not sufficient to generate prices that can serve as valid indicators of the risk of the underlying claims.

5.1.2. Reduction of Transaction Costs

5.1.2.1. The Creditor Bank's Perspective

Besides the dissolution of risk concentrations, some banks on the other hand have successfully economized on transaction costs, esp. those of participation and modification associated with repeated reschedulings and alteration of terms, by actually enhancing the concentration of claims on particular countries. Such a policy has, for instance, been pursued by some US-American banks.

---

111 Cf. section 5.3.1.

112 Cf. p. 74 (section 4.1.1.2.).

Table 16: Ratios of Rescheduling Country Loans to Total Loans at Selected US-Banks[113]

	Total Loans to Rescheduling Countries			
	1985		1987	
Bank	US$ bn.	% of total assets	US$ bn.	% of total assets
Citicorp	15.0	8.6	13.3	6.5
Chase Manhattan	8.9[a]	10.1	8.6	8.7
Bank of America	10.0	8.4	9.3	10.0
Chemical	5.4	9.5	5.9	7.5
J.P. Morgan	5.5[a]	7.9	5.4	7.2
Manufacturers Hanover	9.1[b]	12.0	8.9[b]	2.1
Bankers Trust	n.a.	n.a.	4.0	7.1

----

[a] - Estimate
[b] - Latin America only

Source : *The Economist* [1988].

Table 16 demonstrates that since 1985 these US-American banks - except of Manufacturers Hanover and Bank of America - have reduced their rescheduling country loan holdings relative to total assets by using the secondary market (*The Economist* [1988]). However, by the end of 1985 80% even of Manufacturers Hanover's claims on Latin American debtors were concentrated on only four countries (Brazil, Mexico, Argentina, and Chile). End of 1987 this share almost reached 100% (*ibid.*).

Thus, asset trading has enabled banks to better respond to changes and differences in the subjective valuation of transaction costs associated with loans subject to a particular trade as well as to differences in the amount and structure of total rescheduling country loan holdings (cf. *Guttentag/Herring* [1986b, 271]). As the cost of administrating small exposures almost equals the cost of administrating large exposures, concentration of claims reduces these costs. For smaller US-American and certain European banks with no long-term business interests in particular countries, the secondary market has served as an exit conduit by enabling sales of loans even to the more highly indebted countries. These banks

113 German Banks do not publish their loan claims on individual debtor countries separately.

have primarily been interested in evading the participation and modification costs of continuously rescheduled loans (*Berger* [1988, 124])[114].

Asset trading furthermore enables the reduction of participation costs vis-à-vis supervisory authorities and the general public by circumventing regulatory reporting requirements for specific assets (cf. *Guttentag/Herring* [1986b, 271seq.]). US-American banks, for instance, can in certain cases thereby escape the SEC-rule stipulating to publish separately claims on sovereign borrowers exceeding specified threshold amounts[115]. Parties with preferences for different kinds of exposure as f.i. for claims on the private or the public sector can realize transaction cost savings by using the secondary market to exchange such claims (cf. *ibid.*).

The possibility to charge withholding tax receipts against taxable income under some tax laws enables tax savings for banks under such jurisdictions and allows mutual adaptation of rescheduling country loan positions comprising such receipts with banks in countries where this is not possible[116]. Asset swaps can be beneficial for circumventing potential double taxation of interest income and in cases where a low taxable profit base is insufficient for the absorption of withholding tax obligations. The other bank may perceive benefits when it still has opportunities for such absorption (*Arndt* [1986, 91] and *Ebenroth* [1984, 908]). Hence, both banks can save on taxation-induced participation costs.

The tax laws of the respective domicile countries of banks also determine the extent to which allowances for bad debts are tax deductible and hence account for different valuations of loans that again provide incentives to reduce taxation-induced participation costs through asset trading. For instance, as long as this is

---

114 There is no legally binding obligation to participate in reschedulings. Yet, inter-bank relationships discipline banks to participate and make this endeavour a tedious one.

115 Cf. section 4.1.1.1. Similar regulations that apply to German banks are alluded to on section 4.2.1.1.

116 Cf. *Evans* [1988, 27]. Witholding tax obligations for interest income on individual loans differ relative to the nationality, the legal status of the debtor, and other criteria. The incentive for trading in such assets arises with the opportunity to charge withholding tax that has already been payed against taxable income. The role of witholding tax privileges in Euroloans is treated by *Ebenroth* [1984].

legally possible, non-German banks can be induced to engage in institutional arbitrage by booking some of their rescheduling country loans at their German subsidiaries to benefit from the tax deductibility of specific reserves.

On the other hand, German tax law allows German banks to transfer loans that have been reserved to their foreign subsidiaries or branches. Here, the bank can book possible rescheduling fees and the possibly higher spread on the face value after a rescheduling (cf. *Ebenroth* [1984, 911]). Should the bank sell the loan from its foreign affiliate, eventual gains resulting from the difference of realized price - which could be relatively high after a rescheduling - and book value can also be retained at the affiliate[117].

Information costs are reduced by the communication of negotiated discounts. Although many party-specific factors affect this negotiated result, the discount still conveys some information on the risk perception of a particular debtor country by other market participants. Also, some banks that have expertise in particular types of lending or maintain traditional business relations with particular countries can exploit associated information and participation cost advantages vis-à-vis other banks more extensively (cf. *Guttentag/Herring* [1986b, 271seq.]). This is also a reason why secondary market pricing differentiates between various types of credit products designed for the same borrower under the same agreement.

Furthermore, a bank domiciled in a rescheduling country may use this market to obtain claims against this country because it has a comparative advantage to use the local currency and, thus, may be interested in conversion of the claim into local currency. Such banks can also use asset trades with a large hard currency cash component to more economically respond to liquidity needs (cf. *ibid.*). Participation cost economizing plays an important role for all banks. As many tasks involved in credit management are independent of the amount of the respective loan, banks with lower committments face relatively higher participation costs. Again, the secondary market facilitates the balancing of such incongruities.

Compared to outright securitization of rescheduling country loans the transfer mechanisms actually used in the secondary market may at first glance seem to represent a less efficient form of asset trading. Besides the fact that loan transfers

117 For the conditions applicable to such transactions v. *Arndt* [1986, 109].

require the payment of fees to arrangers and more extensive documentation, different from negotiable instruments, the existing loan contracts contain a complex of clauses that concern the relationship between the creditor banks. However, in the transfer of a negotiable instrument such relationships do not exist. Also, rescheduling agreements usually specify that the creditor has to be a bank or financial institution and thereby restrict the potential investor base (*Yianni/Oakley* [1987, 37]).

However, a major benefit of the original loan relationship between the syndicate members and the borrower is the possibility that, in contrast to the relationship between holders of negotiable securities and the borrower, it does not rule out the option of renegotiation. This renegotiation option is already implied in the syndication mechanism which requires nominal registration of a limited number of members and is not significantly diluted by the existing transfer mechanisms. This is an advantage particularly for banks in the USA where regulatory and accounting institutions like f.i. the 90-day rule have made reschedulings a more efficient means of debt management than capitalization of arrears or conversion of loans into securities.

The greater number of creditors of securitized claims would translate in substantially more costly reschedulings. Also, by this way, adaptation of loan terms to the payment capacity of the debtor is achieved more easily and formal defaults are less likely. Thus, although in the short run modification costs may be lower with securitized instruments, the traditional loan contract mode allows a successive contractual modification that can prevent more detrimental systemic effects. In the past, this helped to avoid substantial threats to the entire world financial system[118,119]. In addition, because of the lack of collateral, the reduced ability to

118 Following *Guttentag/Herring* [1987, 152seq.] four advantages of bank loans versus securitized debt can be identified. Bank loans are a less costly transaction mode when, (1) the analysis of a claims' riskiness, or a borrower's creditworthiness is highly dependent on very subjective information, that may only be obtainable through personal contact, (2) the underlying contract has to be custom-tailored to the needs of the debtor and a special ability or discretion to monitor a borrowers' compliance is required, (3) the funds obtained are required for a specialized project or purpose and/or the collateral used is not perfectly marketable, and when (4) information for risk analysis is partly dependent on the creditor-borrower relationship, because scale economies arise for further lending, further risk analysis, and further monitoring.

bear the costs of extensive debtor information, and the relative advantage of banks in risk diversification, non-bank creditors of securitized claims are generally less able to manage sovereign risks.

Finally, if an increased use of the securitization route is intended this would in most cases necessitate the introduction of some form of factual seniority for such claims. Otherwise, negotiable instruments may not appear attractive to potential outside investors. However, this would conflict with some of the clauses mentioned in section 3.2.3., in particular the negative pledge and the mandatory prepayment clauses. Also, this would presumably imply further decline of secondary market prices which would in turn put further strains on banks' profits. Therefore, comprehensive securitization of rescheduling country loans does still not appear to represent a more efficient tool of debt management than the traditional credit product design from the perspective of banks[120].

5.1.2.2. The Rescheduling Country's Perspective

Discounted secondary market pricing puts borrowing countries at a disadvantage as their debt service is still based on the face value of the debt, not on the market value. I.e., assuming that the price quoted on the secondary market reflects all creditors' valuation of their claims, the actual debt service on that debt exceeds the contractually negotiated debt service. On the other hand, the secondary market offers opportunities for secret buy-back schemes through dummy traders or state-owned banks whereby a country can effectuate a unilateral debt-relief (cf. *Fidler*

---

119 Such modification cost economies can also be expressed in *Williamson's* [1979, 240seq.] words: "*Additional transaction-specific savings can accrue at the interface between supplier and buyer as contracts are successively adapted to unfolding events, and as periodic contract-renewal agreements are reached. Familiarity here permits communication economies to be realized: spezialized language develops as experience accumulates and nuances are signaled and received in a sensitive way. Both institutional and personal trust relations evolve. Thus the individuals who are responsible for adapting the interfaces have a personal as well as an organizational stake in what transpires. Where personal integrity is believed to be operative, individuals located at the interfaces may refuse to be a part of opportunistic efforts to take advantage of (rely on) the letter of the contract when the spirit of the exchange is emasculated. Such refusals can serve as a check upon organizational proclivities to behave opportunistically. Other things being equal, idiosyncratic exchange relations which feature personal trust will survive greater stress and display greater adaptability.*"

120 Cf. also section 5.3.1.

[1989]). Such secret buy-backs may represent violations of the mandatory prepayment and sharing clauses as the seller of a loan in this case is satisfied before the remaining creditors (cf. *Yianni/Oakley* [1987, 39]) but may be tolerated in case of insignificant amounts.

Another benefit lies in the possibility to attain more favorable terms in debt renegotiations when secondary market prices are very low. Also, a country which prefers not to disrupt access to international financial markets may use the secondary market as an instrument to signal its creditworthiness by means of actions that reduce some creditors' enforcement costs such as, e.g., the introduction of a debt equity swap program. On the other hand, by actions that increase creditors' enforcement costs, such as f.i. stopping debt service, the rescheduling country can suppress prices which can eventually lead to substantial debt reduction e.g. through buy-backs (cf. *Franke* [1990]).

5.1.3. Comparative Analysis of Debt Transfer Modes[121]

Depending upon the firm-specific institutional structure of an individual bank, the legal form of a particular asset trade can be chosen from among basically three transfer mechanisms: novation, assignment and participation. In case a bank wants to dispose of a claim completely, novation is the only possible route. Although novation is the most transaction cost-intensive device, only with this mechanism the creditor bank frees itself from any liability to recourse towards the debtor as the entirety of rights and duties of the contract is transferred. The alternative assignment only enables the transfer of duties between assignor and assignee, however omits the approval of the debtor. This makes future claims of the debtor on the assignor that arise from the contract possible and thereby increases participation costs.

To the extent that such claims cannot be avoided, the more burdensome novation is therefore usually preferred to assignment. In case contracts stipulate the approval by all parties of the underlying contract to an assignment agreement, i.e. particularly by the debtor and the guarantor, there are no essential differences between novation and assignment. Such assignments are in effect novations. Even

---

[121] Cf. section 3.1.3. This section draws heavily on *Wulfken/Berger* [1988, 371seq.].

though, most often, not all the parties need to approve the transfer, with increasing secondary market activity, transfers through assignments become more and more standardized and scale economies may lead to increasing adoption of this mechanism.

On the contrary, participation as a much simpler and cheaper form of loan transfer - it does not affect the creditor-debtor relationship - can be a more efficient mechanism when loan transfers are carried out within a banking concern, e.g. for purposes of tax arbitrage by shifting claims between jurisdictions. It merely establishes a contractual relationship between the old creditor and the participant independent from the underlying loan contract. This implies that it is not necessary to create loan loss provisions in anticipation of the difference between face and transfer value of the loan or to write off any portion of the loan.

Furthermore, participations are often an effective conduit for transferring claims outside the contractually defined group of creditor banks, like for example to an international investor that is not a member of the syndicate. However, participations are generally not the appropriate mechanism for preparing debt equity swaps. In order to conduct a debt equity swap, the investor has to be the official owner of the claim. This condition can only be satisfied by a novation or an assignment (cf. *Wulfken* [1989, 120]).

Also, in case no conversion is intended and for conducting transfers between separate banking concerns that are members of the syndicate, participations are not suitable as they increase participation costs by potentially giving rise to future discordances between the old creditor and the participant and the need to coordinate all loan matters and particularly rescheduling exercises with participants in addition to syndicate members (cf. *Bosch* [1985, 154]). By the use of participations, banks can furthermore exacerbate the free rider problem which is often associated with fresh money requirements as now "*each participant may have the right to instruct or veto the position of the contractual creditor in a syndicate vote affecting acceleration, amendment, waiver, or modification of the payment terms*" (*Mudge* [1985, 108]).

5.1.4. Obstacles for Further Efficiency Gains

The range of highly divergent valuations of rescheduling country loans by creditor banks reflected in the difference of the face value of a loan and the complete write-off in a few banks' books, including the price that can be realized through a trade of a similar asset, is not the result of an inefficient secondary market but of an obfuscation caused by the diverse institutional policy determinants of participating banks of different size, specialization and national domicile. This diversity only became apparent after the first de facto defaults of some countries and led to the emergence of such a market in the first place. Such institutional obfuscation therefore both represents the major obstacle for further efficiency improvements and - at the same time - the cause for the emergence of opportunities to increase the efficiency of debt management.

Steps in the direction of further harmonization in order to further efficiency could include the progressive assimilation of hitherto heterogeneous national tax and regulatory laws like for instance a uniform method of charging withholding tax receipts against taxable income. The most important institutional obfuscation among banks' national domiciles, however, is the diversity of possibilities to charge loan loss provisions against taxes. In the case of German banks, a reserve level that is higher than a negotiated discount in an asset sale would lead to the recognition of an extraordinary gain as the difference between the higher price received and the lower book value is taxable. The bank would forgo the interest-free tax credit resulting from the tax deductibility of specific reserves (cf. *Franke* [1989b, 142]).

Particularly in the USA, the lack of unequivocal directions for the accounting and tax treatment of swap transactions, namely the potential of portfolio contamination, prevents an increase of secondary market liquidity. For instance, the largest US banks participate in this market only as brokers but do not trade loans out of their loan portfolios. This institutional impediment is therefore possibly the most important one. Whether this points to overpricing (cf. *GAO* [1988, 29]) or underpricing in the secondary market, however, can only conjectured. Changing the institutional structure by allowing extensive tax deductibility of loan loss reserves would have this opposite effect.

Further standardization and assimilation of national, i.e. primarily New York and English legal conditions of transfer mechanisms could also reduce the participation costs of secondary market transactions and improve tradability and trading volume in the secondary market. Also, the aforementioned diversity of loan valuations could be reduced by such harmonization. Generally, the reduction of transaction costs would have the result that secondary market pricing could more closely reflect individual banks' risk valuation. This could then lead regulators to use secondary market prices as indicators for rescheduling country loan valuation for tax and accounting purposes[122]. Finally, another impediment for further secondary market development is the lack of hedging possibilities.

5.2. DEBT EQUITY SWAPS

A comparative efficiency analysis of debt equity swaps should investigate whether a superior suitability of this financing instrument relative to alternative financing instruments can be identified from the perspective of associated parties. The alternatives considered here are the original loan and foreign direct investment without a secondary market purchase (cf. *Franke* [1989a]). A general efficiency assessment of debt equity swaps, however, is necessarily of little practical avail as the specific institutional conditions of any one transaction may differ substantially from other transactions. Thus, in the following, only the supposedly most notable costs and benefits are confronted. A final conclusion would depend on the subjective evaluation of many basically immeasurable decision variables by the concerned parties and is therefore avoided here. At least at the time of execution of an actual debt equity conversion, it is a valid conjecture that all associated parties perceive some net benefit arising from the transaction. In this sense, it would satisfy the Pareto condition for efficient contracts[123].

---

[122] This line of argument illustrates the mutual feedback character of the relationship between design activities concerning regulatory and market, i.e. organizational, institutions.

[123] Cf. p. 14.

5.2.1. The Creditor Bank's Perspective

As a debt equity swap effectively transforms a debt claim into an equity claim - thus usually allowing for some degree of management control - two main arguments of the transaction cost literature are supported. One is that in case of a high degree of difference of the possession of relevant information among contracting parties, a debt contract is an inferior solution compared to internalization through equity investment. This is because the party with less information will not be able to protect himself (*Hennart* [1989, 215]) and therefore perceive a high level of enforcement costs. Then, this party will either require a higher return or may at some point prefer to switch to an alternative transaction mode (or governance structure), namely a "hierarchical" one - equity investment (cf. *Williamson* [1988, 576]).

The second major argument of a comparable effect of environmental uncertainty or - similarly - institutional obfuscation is also in line with the experience of increasing debt equity swap activity. If the predictability of changes in the environment of the contractual relationship is very low, a large number of outcomes is possible (cf. *Hennart* [1989, 214seq.]). The reason for this mainly lies in highly different institutional frameworks of the contracting parties that exist outside of the behavioral prescriptions of the contract itself. Because of such divergence of institutional determinants of behavior outside of the contract, the respective outside institutions relevant for one party obfuscate the effects of the institutional determinants contained in the contract on that party's behavior from the perspective of the other party. This can result in frequent renegotiation of contracts and, thus, lead to high modification costs.

Again, at some point, one party may prefer to switch to a transaction mode that is expected to exhibit a lower level of enforcement costs - vertical integration through equity investment (cf. *Williamson* [1988, 576]). In both cases, a change in the incentive structure from the debt transaction mode (market relationship) to the equity transaction mode (hierarchical relationship) is regarded as representing an increase in efficiency.

As is true for all debt equity transactions, also in case of a direct debt equity swap conducted by a creditor bank for its own account, an efficiency improvement is highly dependent on the subjective perception of benefits accruing from such asset substitution. If a bank perceives a long-term residual claimant status in a particular industry or corporation of the debtor country which enables direct management control over invested funds as less costly than the original rescheduling country creditor status, it will engage in a debt equity swap. Besides a more favorable ENPV, the associated advantages may also consist of non-quantifiable information and modification cost savings. The same holds for the sale of a loan to an interested investor in the secondary market[124].

From the perspective of creditors, debt equity swaps can reduce enforcement costs, basically information and modification costs. Debt equity swaps provide specific purpose financing instead of the general purpose financing often associated with original loan contracts. Information costs are generally reduced as monitoring is facilitated by achieving a higher degree of discretion of the claimant over protecting or recuperating the asset base of his investment, i.e. over the use of funds[125]. The funds can no longer be absorbed by consumption, capital flight, corruption, and other non-productive uses. The debtor countries, however, may perceive this limitation of their discretion over the use of funds as a disadvantage (cf. *Franke* [1989a, 227]). In fact, debt equity swaps gave rise to reproaches of sovereignty violation by debtor countries.

A bank that perceives an involvement in direct debt equity swap transactions to be a promising route to improve its risk profile is forced to more closely examine the structure and condition of individual enterprises and industries in borrowing countries which may increase information costs in the first place. As long as this is

---

124 Basically the same arguments as in section 5.1.2.1. apply.

125 This holds especially true for the cofinancing of investments together with a development bank - another item on the menu of options. Cofinancing allows commercial banks to share a development bank's credit risk which is lower than the usual risk arising without cofinancing. First, the political clout associated with the support of the sovereign powers which fund the development bank reduces country risk and thus reduces enforcement costs arising from undesired debtor behavior. Second, for the same reason development banks are able to influence and more tightly control all aspects of the implementation of the project. This reduces the commercial risk involved in the project from the perspective of the commercial bank. Hence, information costs can be saved. The development bank benefits by obtaining additional funds to finance worthwile projects it could otherwise not undertake.

in line with the bank's international strategy, however, the ability to obtain and interpret information on relevant decision variables is improved and may then provide information cost advantages for other future business. This benefit, however, primarily accrues to larger global banks, not to small banks.

The explicit inclusion of conversion options in rescheduling agreements reduces the modification costs associated with recovering a maximum of the original loan claims. In case such options have not already been contained in the contract, modification costs would arise because of the need to specifically negotiate for a new transaction and because of greater uncertainty of enforcement. Every additional option for a change of the structure of the contractual relationship contained in the contract offers an additional avenue for enforcement, the existence of which may otherwise be much less certain. Here, however, modification costs are substituted by participation costs. And the decision can then be based on whether these participation costs are less than the modification costs associated with the alternative.

Increased debt equity swap activity presumably benefits creditor banks in three further ways (*Franke* [1989a, 224seq.]). Debt equity swaps create additional demand for rescheduling country debt, thus raising secondary market prices or, at least, contributing to a relatively slower decline of these prices. At the same time, secondary market liquidity is increased. Thereby price volatility is reduced. This, and since debt equity swaps are utilized and supported by creditors, they tend to foster secondary market discounts. The discounts, thus, provide better information f.i. for rescheduling negotiations.

Tax advantages for creditor banks accruing from debt equity swaps do not seem to be of substantial influence in driving up conversion activity. In Germany, tax-deductibility of reserves may even provide a tax induced disincentive for debt equity swaps. In the USA, any secondary market transaction yields a tax relief that results from reporting a loss in the amount of the discount on disposals of loans. Only in as much as in a direct debt equity swap the difference between loan principal and the fair market value of the asset obtained in the exchange is higher than the potential secondary market discount, a tax incentive may exist[126]. The

---

126 Cf. section 4.1.2.2.

same holds for German banks unless the loan has not been written down to a level lower than the fair market value of the asset obtained. However, generalizations are very difficult in this case.

While debt equity swaps increase the potential for economizing on enforcement costs in general, the specific procedures applicable for debt conversion in a particular rescheduling country impact the resulting kind of enforcement costs to be saved. Thus, costs accruing from corruption can be reduced by applying an auction mechanism in assigning the rights for debt conversion to interested investors (*Wulfken* [1989, 183seq.]). Compared to case-by-case approvals of applications for debt conversions by the respective debtor country authorities, this procedure also allows investors a more accurate timing of the investment, thus reducing the risk of price changes. However, from the perspective of the rescheduling country, individual approvals enable greater influence on the direction of foreign investive activity, i.e. on the promotion of particular industries or geographic regions (*ibid.*).

5.2.2. The Investor's Perspective

From the perspective of an investor who has identified an investment opportunity, the debt equity swap mechanism is preferable to another form of investment if it provides investable funds at a lower cost than another form of investment. This depends on the ultimately realizable exchange rate for conversion of the hard currency claim into debtor country currency. This preferential exchange rate for the investor is made possible by the discounts generated in the secondary market risk trading process[127]. However, all differential costs and/or benefits, such as subsidies, additional fees, taxes, and investment restrictions have also to be taken into calculation (cf. *Franke* [1989a, 218seq.]).

5.2.3. The Rescheduling Country's Perspective

The most often cited benefit of debt equity swaps is the reduction of the rescheduling country's external indebtedness. However, if the conversion is financed by long-term local currency debt, the "reduction" of external debt is

---

127 Cf. section 3.3.1.4.

merely a substitution of external debt by internal debt (cf. *Franke* [1989a, 221]. At the same time, the rescheduling country government shifts the default risk onto local citizens. It may be that the government perceives the costs of default to be lower in the latter case.

Also a budget illusion may account for a government's positive attitude towards debt equity swaps. When a country's hard currency obligations are valued at face value at the official exchange rate, a debt equity swap yields a profit in the amount of the discount which the central bank deducts in the exchange of the hard currency claim into local currency, multiplied by the official exchange rate (*Franke* [1989a, 230]). This may entice a rescheduling country government to promote debt equity swaps.

Finally, the implementation of a debt equity conversion program through conveying the commitment to support productive investments can improve the investment climate of a debtor country, thus also enhancing its creditworthiness. It has therefore been argued that debt equity swaps entice foreign investment greater or sooner than could have otherwise been attracted, i.e. that they display "additionality". In a series of interviews with corporate officials, *Bergsman/Edisis* [1988] have found evidence that this is in fact the case. However, whereas this result obtained for virtually all direct swaps by banks, it only obtained for a bit less than half of the multinational corporation investments examined (*ibid.* [v]).

5.2.4. Obstacles for Further Efficiency Gains

The debt relief implied in the execution of a debt equity swap may create a free rider problem for banks supporting debt equity swaps insofar as the reduction of external debt leads to an improvement of a country's servicing capacity for the remaining stock of debt. This may be perceived as beneficial by banks that have a more hesitant attitude towards debt conversions - in most cases the global banks.

Conflicts with stipulations of the underlying loan contracts may pose further problems. F.i. the implementation of a debt equity swap program is made difficult by the need to avoid collision with the mandatory prepayment clause[128]. Also, repatriation restrictions often become necessary elements of debt conversion

---

[128] Cf. section 3.2.3.5. and *Clark/Yianni* [1988, 9 & 13seq.].

programs because of the formal contractual stipulation not to render preferential treatment to any creditor. However, this does not rule out that factual preferential treatment may occur in certain cases. Repatriation restrictions are mostly perceived as a disincentive by debt equity investors. They are aimed at the long-term preservation of the benefits of the investment to the country and at avoiding negative balance of payments effects (cf. *Wulfken* [1989, 195seq.]). However, the scope of these restrictions varies between different countries.

The accounting treatment of debt equity swaps in the USA under established guidelines[129] - although no universal rule exists - will very often lead to the recognition of a loss, thus obstructing the realization of an otherwise attractive investment opportunity as perceived by a bank (cf. *Holzmann* [1989, 18seqq.]). Also, the 45-day advance announcement requirement for certain debt equity swap investments by US banks represents a competitive disadvantage relative to private investors or banks of other jurisdictions (*Rubinstein* [1988, 177])[130].

As is true for any foreign investment, also debt equity swapping will cause inflation to rise if the local currency needed for the exchange of large amounts of hard currency claims is generated through money creation. The issuance of long-term government bonds, as successfully implemented in Chile for example, can substantially retard such effects. However, this may in turn affect interest rates. Another argument voiced by debtor countries against debt equity swaps concerns the fear of a violation of sovereignty.

Finally, from the perspective of debtor countries, the potential of "round-tripping" represents a disadvantage. As a debt equity conversion program implies the establishment of at least two exchange rates, arbitrage opportunities arise. An investor may use the local currency obtained under the preferential debt equity swap rate to purchase hard currency at the official rate. This amount can in turn be used to convert a higher amount of hard currency debt at the debt equity swap rate and so on. This process would lead to a gradual depletion of hard currency reserves of the debtor country (cf. *Roberts/Remolona* [1987, 51]).

---

129 Cf. section 4.1.3.4.

130 Cf. section 4.1.1.8.

Also the potential of moral hazard by the debtor country may prevent creditors from promoting debt equity swaps. Debtor country governments may perceive an incentive to reduce the secondary market price of their debt as this would allow to deduct a larger discount in converting their hard currency debt into local currency. This enables the debtor country to save on local currency for equal amounts of foreign currency (*Franke* [1989a, 224]).

5.3. OTHER DEBT REDUCTION MODES

5.3.1. Debt for Debt Swaps

Besides debt for debt swaps that are undertaken within the context of asset trading (v.s.), concerted debt for debt swaps are conducted only as part of debt renegotiation exercises. Particularly securitization of rescheduling country debt deserves mentioning, as this conversion mode is often intended to reflect secondary market valuation and to offer even higher transaction cost advantages[131]. The most prominent case examples so far have been the Mexican conversions of 1988 and 1990[132].

---

131 Therefore other debt for debt swap modes such as relending and currency redenomination are not focussed on here. The main benefits of relending - like of onlending - are that it allows banks to avoid the restraining effect of lending limit regulations and help them to start or continue business relations with specific customers in rescheduling countries as well as to fund subsidiaries by conducting debt equity swaps with onlendable claims. Currency redenomination improves possibilities for exchange risk management by creditor banks.

132 In 1988, an unexpectedly low amount of US$ 1.108 billion, i.e. about 30% of US$ 3.67 billion of old debt accepted for conversion, could be deducted from Mexico's total external debt (*Ebenroth/Messer* [1988, 492] and *Stausberg* [1988]). In 1990, the debt principal reduction amounted to US$ 6.4 billion (*Truell* [1990]). This was achieved within a three part restructuring of US$ 48 billion of old commercial bank debt. It consisted (1) of a conversion of about US$ 19 billion into bonds with a principal reduced by 35%, (2) of a conversion of about US$ 24 billion into bonds carrying a low interest rate of 6¼%, and (3) for the remaining part of about US$ 4.8 billion some banks committed to new lending of 25% of their medium- and long-term loans outstanding. The agreement was reached only with substantial support by the US government (cf. *ibid.*).

The effects of debt reduction by debt for debt swaps on banks depend very much on the applicable accounting treatment. Immediate loss recognition would lead banks with a high exposure to the respective country to regard this debt reduction mode as disadvantageous. The simultaneous offer in conjunction with other conversion options (cf. n. 132), however, provides various types of creditor banks with the opportunity to choose the type of transaction mode most consistent both with its long-term business strategy and its financial capacity. This helps banks to save on information, participation, and modification costs.

In case both principal and interest of the bonds are collateralized, also modification costs are substantially reduced as the security can readily be traded in a secondary market and because bonds reduce the potential of intercreditor conflicts associated with syndicated loans as they usually do not contain clauses such as the sharing and mandatory prepayment clause. In the case of default the risk of non-payment is shifted from the rescheduling country to the issuer of the collateral. This would, however, also require demand by non-bank investors which will help to increase the liquidity of the secondary market. In any case, a comparative efficiency analysis between securitization and loan trading is also highly dependent on the unique combination of many institutional influences on an individual bank and a general conclusion is therefore of little avail. Should the bonds used in such conversions exempt holders from future new lending requests (exit bonds), the associated free rider problem[133] can significantly be resolved and further modification cost savings can be achieved.

In case the principal and/or interest of the negotiable debt instrument is lower than the original debt for which it is exchanged - as has been the case in the Mexican conversion of 1990 -, these securitization modes result in effective reduction of rescheduling countries' external debt. Given that these countries pursue adequate macroeconomic and structural policies, this, in turn, may support progress in overall economic rehabilitation and thereby also improve a country's creditworthiness. An additional relative benefit is that compared to debt equity swaps, debt for bond swaps do not cause inflationary pressures in the debtor country.

---

133 Cf. section 2.3.2.3.

New lending and conversions could be spurred by giving priority to those lenders willing to participate. A main institutional obstacle for implementing debt for debt swap schemes is that the unavoidable introduction of seniority of securitized claims contradicts the pari passu and negative pledge clause. A waiver of these clauses usually requires unanimity among creditor banks. For this reason such seniority has to be de facto rather than de jure (*Williamson* [1988, 27]). In the case of the Mexican debt for bond conversion of February 1988, a waiver of the pari passu covenant had been agreed upon by a majority of creditors in order to implement the scheme (cf. *Ebenroth/Cremer* [1988, 489seq.]).

In the early years of sovereign debt repayment problems, the homogeneity of treatment of syndicate members by means of several clauses has been perceived as a successful innovation. This was because these clauses - especially the cross-default clause - increased the cost of default for borrowers, reduced enforcement costs for lenders and may therefore have prevented large-scale repudiations (cf. *Folkerts-Landau* [1985, 327passim]). This contractual principle, however, is now increasingly perceived as an obstacle for the implementation of different menu items that would better correspond with the diverging interests of many individual bank creditors. This particularly applies to securitization.

When the new debt instruments obtained in a debt for debt swap imply the exemption of the creditor from future restructurings, like f.i. exit bonds do, the volume of "inflexible" debt is increased. Therefore, in reducing debt and debt service of rescheduling countries, it is important to reach a level of debt that is sustainable in the long-run without necessitating further restructurings (*World Bank* [1989, 4]).

5.3.2. Debt Buy-Backs

From the perspective of the creditor banks, any asset, in this case cash, that provides for a reduction or even elimination of any further enforcement costs associated with the original claims will subjectively be valued higher than the existing claim. In case a bank values its outstanding claims at 50% of par it will accept to exchange this debt for any amount of cash greater than 50% of par. *Krugman* [1989, 44] has indicated, that an efficiency assessment of buy-backs would depend to some extent on the source of the funds used to buy back the loans in question.

Given that the amount of cash to be used in the buy-back is already at the disposal of the country, a buy-back of the claims of one creditor puts the remaining creditors at a disadvantage. Despite a nominal reduction of the country's external debt, enforcement costs of the remaining creditors are increased further. This is the case as long as the country is not deemed to fully abide by its future debt service and repayment duties, which is indicated by a secondary market price of less than par. The remaining banks may thereby perceive to indirectly pay for the transaction considered to be beneficial by the country and the other creditor.

Given that the amount needed to execute the partial buy-back is provided by some third party, as, e.g., by an international organization, the result is not much different in principle. However, both the creditors that sell back their debt for a price higher than the subjective value they attach to this debt and the creditors that hold on to their claims realize enforcement cost savings when the buy-back is conducted at par and the debtor's remaining reserves suffice for complete satisfaction of the remaining creditors. For the first group all further enforcement costs associated with the underlying contract are eliminated because these banks completely escaped from the contractual relationship. The second group is better off because the country can now be expected to repay its obligations in full.

However, if the partial buy-back is conducted at a price of less than par, once it is known that third party funds are available for this purpose, the situation becomes comparable to the situation when funds are entirely at the disposal of the debtor country in the first place. Then, the debtor country's creditworthiness can be considered to have improved at the time of the availability of third party funds. Its total debt is reduced by the nominal amount corresponding to the buy-back. In both of these cases of external buy-backs the creditors as well as the rescheduling country gain at the expense of the source of third party funds - f.i. governments of industrial countries.

A drawback of the establishment of an IMF/World Bank funded buy-back facility, as proposed for such purposes by the US government under the "Brady Plan", lies in the inflationary effects of the potential money creation by industrial country governments. Another more significant obstacle for partial buy-backs, particularly when financed by the rescheduling country itself, is a collision with the mandatory prepayment, sharing and pari passu clauses contained in existing credit agreements. Thus, a condition for conducting a comprehensive buy-back is the consent of creditors. Because of the free rider phenomenon mentioned and the differing preferences of banks such consent is conceivable only in the case of small amounts of debt.

5.3.3. Debt for Nature and Debt for Development Swaps

From the perspective of banks, compared to secondary market debt sales, both debt for nature and debt for development swaps, if conducted by way of donations[134], are not attractive under current institutional conditions. Whereas in the first case a bank would receive the secondary market price in cash and would receive a tax deduction on the associated loss, in the second case with a charitable contribution it would only receive the tax deduction on the face value of the debt donated. A benefit may accrue to the bank from public demonstration of benevolence which, however, may not outweigh the costs incurred.

Swaps that are conducted through a purchase of debt on the secondary market require the prior raising of funds by the respective conservation agency which again depends on charitable contributions by third parties.

A participation cost barrier for implementation of debt for nature swaps is the necessity to obtain a waiver of the mandatory prepayment and sharing clause of the underlying loan contract. Most recently this problem has been circumvented by so-called "back-to-back" transactions (cf. *Ebenroth/Bühler* [1990]). These are agreements without explicit contractual specifications that require the participating bank to completely forgive a particular debt claim in exchange for the debtor country government's commitment to fund a particular conservation measure. No prior transfer of the loan is required. Instead of an explicit legally enforceable contract, an implicit party-enforced contract is used.

Whereas enforcement costs may already be very high in case of explicit contracts as a consequence of potential difficulties to compel the debtor country government to abide by the agreements, they may be even more pronounced with implicit

---

[134] Cf. section 4.1.2.4.

contracts of the back-to-back type. However, actual enforcement by judicial means may in any case never be a valid measure. In addition, fears of sovereignty violation may also pose a barrier to more extensive use of debt for nature and debt for development swaps.

Another major obstacle for debt for nature and also debt for development swaps are inflationary effects. Often, a significant amount of time elapses between the conversion of the hard currency claim into local currency funds and the actual investment in the respective conservation or development measure. In high inflation countries this can represent a significant loss for the implementing agency. In addition, like with debt equity swaps, inflationary effects may result from the conversion itself. However, amounts converted in debt for nature swaps are usually insignificantly small and inflationary effects can, in any case, be mitigated by issuing local currency bonds.

A free rider problem can be associated with debt for nature swaps as the creditor banks and the conservation organization bear the costs of debt reduction whereas the long-term benefits may accrue to literally everyone (cf. *Rauscher* [1989, 65]). As long as the subjective cost/benefit analysis of participating banks is still in favor of debt for nature conversions, this externality is negligible. However, the institutionalization of some compensation scheme that provides monetary incentives to creditor banks and conservation organizations may significantly spur further debt for nature conversions. Such a scheme could be established at an international agency and could be financed by the members of this agency. The same argument applies to debt for development swaps.

5.3.4. Debt for Commodity Swaps

A Debt for commodity swap is an appropriate transaction mode for a bank that maintains a significant goods trading operation itself. Only in this case, the participation costs associated with marketing the goods in question may be less than the participation and modification costs associated with holding on to the old claim. Generally, only non-traditional goods are involved in debt for commodity swaps. Hence, rescheduling countries can benefit from an additional marketing network which may otherwise not be available and promote products traditionally not included in its exports. Also, the country can generate additional export revenues because the amount of the goods sold usually exceeds the amount of the debt retired.

Major obstacles of debt for commodity swaps lie in the possibly low quality of the goods provided and, thus, the problem to identify adequate suppliers in the country (cf. *Chamberlin/Gruson/Weltchek* [1988, 458]). In addition, a conflict with the sharing clause of the underlying loan agreement may also prevent debt for commodity swaps unless the amounts of debt involved are perceived to be insignificant.

5.4. SUMMARY

The categorization of innovations commonly used distorts a little some common features of all debt reduction modes. Except of debt for nature and debt for development swaps one important commonality lies in the fact that in all cases the original creditor exchanges an existing loan asset with another asset. Exactly which asset is preferable to alternative assets depends on the relative size of enforcement costs associated with the respective transaction modes. These, again, depend on the particular institutional determinants of individual banks. Here, both firm- and sector-specific determinants combine to form a multitude of different enforcement cost perceptions among creditor banks.

Among the major firm-specific determinants are the long-term business strategy of a bank concerning rescheduling countries. This and the financial capacity to absorb losses associated with some of these transcations affects a bank's principal attitude towards secondary market and debt reduction transactions. Other existing business focusses and the capacity to set up an organizational structure which would allow to engage in some of the innovative transactions, like, e.g., asset trading units, determines to some extent which assets are preferred in conversions.

A major sector-specific product-related impediment for the implementation of measures to reduce banks' enforcement costs are the clauses contained in the underlying contracts. All debt reduction transactions that are negotiated individually between a creditor and the rescheduling country, i.e. all swaps that have not explicitly been covered in rescheduling agreements like in the case of debt that has been designed as eligible for debt equity swaps, potentially conflict with the sharing clause, and in case payment is effected in the currency of the original loan contract, also with the mandatory prepayment provision.

With debt for debt swaps conducted by individual banks in the secondary market conflicts with stipulations of the underlying contract can be overcome by choosing the adequate transfer mode. Securitization as part of debt renegotiations has proven to conflict with the negative pledge clause. However, here specifically negotiated waivers of this clause offer an escape.

In addition, sector-specific regulations - as introduced in section 4. - pose important additional determinants for banks' behavior. Besides the respective conversion regulations in debtor countries particularly tax and accounting regulations can provide crucial incentives or disincentives for engaging in rescheduling country debt transactions.

Besides the indirect effects mentioned in section 5.1.2.2. secondary market transactions themselves do not have a significant impact on the economies of rescheduling countries. The effects of debt reduction transactions on the debtor country, however, depend very much on the source of the assets used in the exchange. Although the total amount of debt may be reduced, other effects may not be desired. F.i., should the reduction involve payment of local currency, like in the case of debt equity swaps, inflation may be increased.

Because of the combined effect of this complex of many institutional influences generalized statements about the preferability of particular transaction modes over other transaction modes are not possible. Rather, in order to take account of the resulting divergence of interests of creditor banks and the different needs and capacities of rescheduling countries, a combination of secondary market and concerted actions will provide for further progress on a case-by-case basis. First, the emergence of the secondary market, and second, the successful development of new debt reduction modes like debt equity swaps, concerted debt for debt swaps, buy-backs and debt for nature swaps are topical examples for the need of such mutual dependence of two fundamental nonexclusive forms of organizing economic transactions - markets and long-term hierarchical relationships which are both based on contracts.

6. CONCLUSIONS

The guiding assumption of this study has been that innovations in international debt management are intended to minimize commercial banks' transaction costs associated with rescheduling country lending. After the occurrence of many de facto defaults - without triggering de jure defaults -, particularly enforcement cost minimization became the relevant objective. Another objective for the design of these innovations could be viewed in the restoration of creditworthiness of rescheduling countries (cf. *IIF* [1987]). This objective, however, can be considered secondary as access to significant future new lending is not conceivable without any means of effective enforceability of debt claims.

Within a nine-year process of continued contractual readjustment, a number of innovative credit product designs gradually emerged on the basis of the major organizational innovation in the course of the debt crisis - a secondary market for rescheduling country loans. This market brought about the possibility to value outstanding claims at prices below face value which reflects the enforcement costs incurred by creditor banks. Secondary market asset trading enabled the implementation of debt conversion products which allowed creditors to reduce enforcement costs by engaging in institutional arbitrage and, at the same time, also led to some reduction of rescheduling countries' external commercial bank debts. Among these products are debt equity swaps, debt for debt swaps, debt for nature and debt for development swaps.

In analyzing their comparative efficiency, a central explanatory factor for the highly heterogeneous enforcement cost perceptions among creditor banks has turned out to be the sector-specific regulatory influence on rescheduling country lending and secondary market decisions. Apart from firm-specific institutional and political factors, these play a major role for understanding the efficiency of the secondary market based product innovations. A detailed analysis of the most relevant regulatory influences for US banks - the dominant players in debt crisis management - has been provided in chapter 4. For comparative purposes, also the relevant German institutions have been considered.

The most important regulatory influence in this respect results from the supervisory, tax, and accounting rules concerning the valuation of rescheduling country debt. Here, the major result is that particularly the tax treatment of provisions for potential loan-losses has very constraining effects on US banks' net income, compared to the German practice. Such divergence of tax regulations in different creditor bank jurisdictions has led to a differentiation of banks' willingness to engage in secondary market trading and therefore contributed to the emergence of trading opportunities in the first place.

The study also served to highlight the mutual feedback relationships between institutional design decisions of bankers and regulators. Although economic forces may have triggered the payment difficulties of rescheduling countries - these, however, ultimately also depend on political decision making which follows institutionalized criteria - the actual design of innovations intended to reduce the associated enforcement costs for banks is a direct reflection of the preexisting institutional framework. Regulators, in turn, may respond to the emergence of new product, organizational, or procedural institutions by innovating sector-specific legal institutions. A case in point would be the amendment of Regulation K designed to spur debt equity swapping by US banks.

Bank supervisory rules under this institutional perspective may be enacted to enhance the safety of the financial sector by prescribing risk reducing norms of behavior or relieving participants from strains with detrimental systemic effects. However, as long as such actions are confined to one national financial sector, on an international level they may entice innovative arbitrage behavior by banks leading to new, usually more complex risk/reward relationships (cf. *Bleeke/Bryan* [1988, 36]). From a transaction cost perspective, further international harmonization of supervisory, tax, and accounting institutions accross national jurisdictions would therefore contribute to developing the perception of increased stability and efficiency.

The perception of sector-specific institutions as barriers for transactions leads banks to search for an institutional framework that allows them greater discretion over the pursuit of firm-specific objectives. This search will eventually lead to the emergence of innovations, in particular product innovations. Such processes of institutional arbitrage accross jurisdictions lead to an increasing globalization of financial culture (cf. *ibid.*). The enforcement problems of rescheduling country loans, however, represent a phenomenon that puts into question the ability of individual banks to successfully overcome institutional obfuscation by the help of firm-specific innovations. This points to the need for new international sector-specific ramifications for less-industrialized country financing. For instance, the lack of an effective international bankruptcy institution which could take on some of the associated potential enforcement costs obstructs the possibility of future new lending from private sources significantly[135].

Less-industrialized country debt issues are obviously prone to institutional obfuscation. This is not only the result of the various firm- and sector-specific institutional divergences of various national cultures and jurisdictions, but may also be due to the lack of an institutionalized forum or journal devoted to international interdisciplinary research on sovereign debt, combining economic, legal, sociological, and political science contributions. Considering the forthcoming transition of the debt crisis into a financing crisis and the myriad of articles of lawyers, economists, bankers and others which are dispersed over some hundred publications, this may represent an efficient innovative institutional arrangement.

---

135 See also *Sachs* [1989c, 245]. An opinion survey among some 600 European experts published in 1986 yielded the result that European banks will not be prepared to increase their lending exposure to less-industrialized countries (*Arthur Andersen & Co.*, [1986, 54]).

REFERENCES

Agmon, Tamir and J.K. **Dietrich** (1983). International Lending and Income Redistribution. An Alternative View of Country Risk. *Journal of Banking and Finance* 7, 483-495.

Alchian, Armen A. and Harold **Demsetz** (1972). Production, Information Costs, and Economic Organization. *American Economic Revue*, 62, 777-795.

Alchian, Armen A. and Harold **Demsetz** (1973). The Property Rights Paradigm. *Journal of Economic History*, Vol. XXXIII, 16-27.

Allen, Mark **et al.** (1989). International Capital Markets. Developments and Prospects. By a Staff Team from the Exchange and Trade Relations and Research Departments. World Economic and Financial Surveys, April, Washington, D.C.: International Monetary Fund.

American Institute of Certified Public Accountants "**AICPA**" (1984). Audits of Banks. Industry Audit Guide. Prepared by the Banking Committee, 2nd ed., Including Statement of Position Issued by the Accounting Standards Division. New York.

American Law Institute (1981). Restatement of the Law Second, Contracts 2d, Vols. 2 and 3. St. Paul, Minn.: American Law Institute Publishers.

Arndt, Andreas (1986). Die Besteuerung internationaler Geschäftstätigkeit deutscher Banken. Schriften des Instituts für ausländisches und internationales Finanz- und Steuerwesen der Universität Hamburg, Bd. 9. Baden-Baden: Nomos.

Arpan, Jeffrey S. and Lee H. **Radebaugh** (1981). International Accounting and Multinational Enterprise. Boston: Warren, Gorham & Lamont.

Arrow, Kenneth (1974). The Limits of Organization. New York: W.W. Norton.

Arthur Andersen & Co. (1985). The Decade of Change. Banking in Europe - the next ten years. London.

Ayitttey, George B.N. (1986). The Real Foreign Debt Problem. *Wall Street Journal*, April 8.

Bank for International Settlements "**BIS**" (1986). Recent Innovations in International Banking. April. Basel.

Bank for International Settlements "**BIS**" (1987). Proposals for international convergence of capital measurement and capital standards. Committee on Banking Regulations and Supervisory Practices, Consultative paper, December. Basel.

Bank für Internationalen Zahlungsausgleich "**BIZ**" (1987). Vorschläge zu einer internationalen Konvergenz der Eigenkapitalmessung und Eigenkapitalanforderungen. Ausschuss für Bankenbestimmungen und -überwachung, Konsultationspapier, Dezember. Basel. Unpublished.

Bardos, Jeffrey (1987). The Risk-based Capital Agreement: A Further Step towards Policy Convergence. *Federal Reserve Bank of New York Quarterly Review*, Winter 1987-88, 26-34.

Baumann, Martin F. (1987). Statement before the Subcommittee on International Finance, Trade and Monetary Policy of the Committee on Banking, Finance and Urban Affairs, March 10. In: Banking Committee Provisions of the Trade Bill. Hearings before the Subcommittee on International Finance, Trade and Monetary Policy of the Committee on Banking, Finance and Urban Affairs. U.S. House of Representatives. 100th Congress, 1st session on Title IV of H.R. 3. A Bill to Enhance the Competitiveness of American Industry and for Other Purposes. March 3,4 and 10. Serial No. 100-6, Washington, D.C.: U.S. Government Printing Office, 387-396 and 419-429.

Baumann, Martin F. and J. Richard **Harvey**, Jr. (1989). LDC Debt Strategies: Accounting and Tax Issues. *Bank Accounting & Finance*, Vol. 2, 4, Summer, 3-16.

Bench, Robert A. (1987). The Regulatory Environment for Debt/Equity Swaps. In: Proceedings of the Euromoney Debt/Equity Swaps Conference, New York City, March 11-13, 1987. Euromoney: London. Unpublished. 9-12.

Benston, George J. **et al.** (1986). Perspectives on Safe & Sound Banking. Past, Present and Future. A Study Commissioned by the American Bankers Association. Cambridge, MA: The MIT Press.

Berger, Klaus Peter (1989). Die Eigenkapitalausstattung der Banken nach neuem EG-Recht. *Betriebs-Berater*, H.15, 30.5., 1017-1022.

Berger, Walter (1988). Neue Ansätze im Schuldenmanagement für Entwicklungsländer. *Sparkasse*, 105. Jg., 3, 123-129.

Bergsman, Joel and Wayne **Edisis** (1988). Debt-Equity Swaps and Foreign Direct Investment in Latin America. International Finance Corporation, Discussion Paper No. 2. Washington, D.C.: The World Bank.

Birck, Heinrich und Heinrich **Meyer** (1977). Die Bankbilanz. Handkommentar, 3. Aufl., 2. Teillieferung. Wiesbaden: Gabler.

Bleeke, Joel A. and Lowell L. **Bryan** (1988). The globalization of financial markets. *The McKinsey Quarterly*, Winter, 17-38.

Bogdanowicz-Bindert, Christine A. and Paul **Sacks** (1984). The Role of Information: Closing the Barn Door? In: Feinberg, Richard E. and Valeriana Kallab (eds.). Uncertain Future: Commercial Banks and the Third World. U.S.-Third World Policy Perspectives, No. 2. Washington, D.C.: Overseas Development Council, 69-78.

Börsenzeitung (1987). Sammelwertberichtigung. 13. Oktober.

Bosch, Ulrich (1985). Vertragliche Regelungen in internationalen Kreditverträgen als risikopolitisches Instrument. Erfahrungen im Licht der jüngsten Länderumschuldungen. In: Krümmel, Hans-Jacob (Hrsg.). Internationales Bankgeschäft. *Supplements to Kredit und Kapital*, 8, Berlin: Duncker & Humblot, 117-159.

Bradfield, Michael and Nancy R. Jacklin (1984). The Problems Posed by Negative Pledge Covenants in International Loan Agreements. *Columbia Journal of Transnational Law*, Vol. 23, 131-142.

Breeden, Charles H. and Peter G. **Toumanoff** (1985). Transactions Costs and Economic Institutions. In: Leube, Kurt R. and Albert H. Zlabinger (eds.). The Political Economy of Freedom. Essays in Honor of F.A. Hayek. München: Philosophia.

Bruner, Robert and John M. **Simms**, Jr. (1987). The International Debt Crisis and Bank Security Returns. *Journal of Money, Credit, and Banking*, 1, 46-55.

Buchanan, James M. (1984). Rights, Efficiency, and Exchange: The Irrelevance of Transaction Cost. In: Neumann, Manfred (Hrsg.). Ansprüche, Eigentums- und Verfügungsrechte. Arbeitstagung des Vereins für Socialpolitik, Gesellschaft für Wirtschafts- und Sozialwissenschaften in Basel 1983. Schriften des Vereins für Socialpolitik, Gesellschaft für Wirtschafts- und Sozialwissenschaften, Neue Folge, Bd. 140. Berlin: Duncker & Humblot, 9-24.

Buchheit, Lee C. and Ralph **Reisner** (1988). The Effect of the Sovereign Debt Restructuring Process on Inter-Creditor Relationships. *University of Illinois Law Review*, 2, 493-517.

Budäus, Dietrich (1988). Theorie der Verfügungsrechte als Grundlage der Effizienzanalyse öffentlicher Regulierung und öffentlicher Unternehmen. In: Budäus, Dietrich, Elmar Gerum und Gebhard Zimmermann (Hrsg.). Betriebswirtschaftslehre und Theorie der Verfügungsrechte. Wiesbaden: Gabler.

Büschgen, Hans E. (1987). Controlling und Marketing. In: Krumnow, Jürgen und Matthias Metz (Hrsg.). Rechnungswesen im Dienste der Bankpolitik. Stuttgart: C.E. Poeschel, 159-180.

Calamari, John D. and Joseph M. **Perillo** (1977). Contracts. 2. ed., St. Paul, Minn.: West Publishing Co.

Chamberlin, Michael, Michael **Gruson** and Paul **Weltchek** (1988). Sovereign Debt Exchanges. *University of Illinois Law Review*, 2, 415-480.

Cheshire, Geoffrey C., Cecil H.F. **Fifoot** and Michael P. **Furmston** (1986). Law of Contract. 11. ed. London: Butterworths.

Clark, Keith and Andrew **Yianni** (1988). Are there solutions to the debt problem? *International Financial Law Review*, September, 9-14.

Cline, William R. (1987). Mobilizing Bank Lending to Debtor Countries. Policy Analyses in International Economics, 18, June. Institute for International Economics, Washington, D.C.

Cline, William R. (1987). Mobilizing Bank Lending to Debtor Countries. Policy Analyses in International Economics, 18, June. Institute for International Economics, Washington, D.C.

Cohen, Benjamin J. (1986). In Whose Interest? International Banking and American Foreign Policy. A Council on Foreign Relations Book. New Haven: Yale University Press.

Commons, John R. (1990/1934). Institutional Economics. Its Place in Political Economy. Vol. One, with a New Introduction by Malcolm Rutherford. New Brunswick: Transaction Publishers. Originally published New York: Macmillan.

Conover, C.T., William M. **Isaac**, and Paul A. **Volcker** (1983). Joint Memorandum. April 7. In: Proposed Solutions to the International Debt Crisis. Hearing before the Committee on Banking, Finance and Urban Affairs. United States Senate. 98th Congress, 1st session on S. 502 and S. 692. April 11, Washington, D.C.: U.S. Government Printing Office, 23-52.

Cornell, Bradford and Alan C. **Shapiro** (1986). The Reaction of Bank Stock Prices to the International Debt Crisis. *Journal of Banking and Finance*, 10, 55-73.

Cuddington, John T. (1986). Capital Flight: Estimates, Issues, and Explanations. *Princeton Studies in International Finance*, 58, December. Princeton: Princeton University.

Dale, Richard (1984). The Regulation of International Banking. Cambridge: Woodhead-Faulkner.

Damm, Gabriele, Gerhard **Friedla** und Reinhard H. **Schmidt** (1987). Eine Effizienzanalyse zinsvariabler Finanzierungsinstrumente. *Zeitschrift für betiebswirtschaftliche Forschung*, 39. Jg., 2, 146-162.

Darity, William A., Jr. and Bobbie L. **Horn** (1988). The Loan Pushers. The Role of Commercial Banks in the International Debt Crisis. Cambridge, MA: Ballinger.

Delamaide, Darrell (1983). West Germany: Something to brag about. *Euromoney*, April, 79-80.

Delamaide, Darrell **et al.** (1983). How good are bad loan reserves? *Institutional Investor*, April 1983, 77-89.

Demsetz, Harold (1964). The Exchange and Enforcement of Property Rights. *Journal of Law and Economics*, 7, 11-26.

Deppe, Hans-Dieter (1987). Finanzielle Haftung heute - Obsoletes Relikt oder markwirtschaftliche Fundamentalleistung. In: Claussen, Carsten P., Lothar Hübl und Hans-Peter Schneider (Hrsg.) (1987). Zweihundert Jahre Geld und Brief. Herausforderungen an die Kapitalmärkte. Festgabe an die Niedersächsische Börse zu Hannover aus Anlaß ihres 200jährigen Bestehens. Frankfurt am Main: Fritz Knapp Verlag, 179-204.

Deutsche Bank AG (1989). Geschäftsbericht für das Jahr 1988. Frankfurt am Main.

Deutsche Bundesbank (1989). Statistische Beihefte zu den Monatsberichten der Deutschen Bundesbank. Reihe 3, Juli. Frankfurt am Main.

Dornbusch, Rüdiger (1986). Dollars, Debts, and Deficits. Cambridge, MA., and Leuven: MIT Press and Leuven University Press.

Drumm, Hans Jürgen (1990). Coordination. In: Grochla, Erwin et al. (eds.). Handbook of German Business Management. Stuttgart: C.E Poeschel and Berlin: Springer, 570-579.

Eaton, Jonathan and Lance **Taylor** (1986). Developing Country Finance and Debt. *Journal of Development Economics*, 22, 209-265.

Eaton, Jonathan, Mark **Gersovitz** and Joseph E. **Stiglitz** (1986). The Pure Theory of Country Risk. *European Economic Review*, 30, 481-513.

Ebenroth, Carsten Thomas (1984). Zu den Grenzen der Besteuerung von Banken im Eurokreditgeschäft. *Juristen Zeitung*, 39. Jg., H. 20, 19. Oktober, 907-912.

Ebenroth, Carsten Thomas (1988). Internationale Verschuldungskrise - Lösungsansätze und unternehmerische Chancen aus der Sicht der Landesbanken. Vortrag vor Firmenkunden des Regionalbereichs Düsseldorf der Westdeutschen Landesbank Girozentrale am 29. September 1988 in Düsseldorf. Düsseldorf: Westdeutsche Landesbank Girozentrale.

Ebenroth, Carsten Thomas (1989). Die internationalprivatrechtliche Anknüpfung von Finanzinnovationen aus deutscher und schweizerischer Sicht. In: Festschrift für Max Keller zum 65. Geburtstag. Zürich: Schulthess.

Ebenroth, Carsten Thomas und Stefan **Bühler** (1990). Verschuldungskrise und Umweltschutz - Debt-for-Nature Swaps, eine Lösung für zwei Probleme. *Natur und Recht*, **forthcoming**.

Ebenroth, Carsten Thomas und Matthias **Cremer** (1988). Mexikos Umschuldungsangebot: Ein Ansatz zur Lösung der Schuldenkrise? *Die Bank*, 9, 488-494.

The Economist (1988). On debt row. April 2, 1988, 70.

Epperlein, Joachim (1987). Germany. In: Ernst & Whinney (ed.). International Bank Accounting. 2nd ed. London: Euromoney, 137-164.

Eskridge, William N. Jr. (ed.) (1985). A Dance Along the Precipice. The Political and Economic Dimensions of the International Debt Problem. Lexington, MA.: Lexington Books.

Evans, Richard (1988). Anomalous but profitable. *Euromoney*, January. Special Supplement: Global Debt, 25-31.

Falcoff, Mark (1986). Peruvian President Gnaws Away his Northern Lifeline. *Wall Street Journal*, March 28.

Faria, Eduardo C.G. de, J. Andrew **Stott** and Nigel J.C. **Buchanan** (1988). PW/Euromoney Debt-Equity Swap Guide. Special Report. London: Euromoney.

Federal Financial Institutions Examination Council "**FFIEC**" (1989; 1988; 1987; 1986; 1985; 1983). Country Exposure Lending Survey: December 1988, 1987, 1986, 1985, 1984, and 1982 (various issues). Washington D.C.

Federal Reserve Bulletin (1989). Final Rule - Amendment to Regulations H and Y. March, 156-187.

Fidler, Stephen (1989). Third World debt traders: the unresolved mystery. *Financial Times*, December 19, 1989, 18.

Finance & Development (1983). Debt rescheduling: what does it mean? September, 26-30.

Finneran, G.B. (1987). The Practice of Debt/Equity Swaps. In: Debt/Equity Conversion: A Strategy for Easing Third World Debt. Proceedings of a Conference Sponsored by the Heritage Foundation Center for International Economic Growth, January 21, 1987. Washington, D.C., 27-35.

Fischer, Stanley (1988). Economic Development and the Debt Crisis. In: Dräger, Christian and Lothar Späth (Hrsg.). Internationales Währungssystem und weltwirtschaftliche Entwicklung. Eine Herausforderung an die internationale Wirtschaftskooperation. Dokumentation des Malenter Symposions VII. Edition Dräger-Stiftung Zukunft, Bd. 12. Baden-Baden: Nomos, 177-194.

Folkerts-Landau, David (1985). The Changing Role of International Bank Lending in Development Finance. *International Monetary Fund Staff Papers*, Vol. 32, 2, June, 317-363.

Franke, Günter (1987a). Organisation und Regulierung internationaler Finanzmärkte. In: Kapitalmarkt und Finanzierung, Jahrestagung des Vereins für Socialpolitik, Gesellschaft für Wirtschafts-und Sozialwissenschaften in München 1986, Schriften des Vereins für Socialpolitik, Neue Folge Band 165. Berlin: Duncker & Humblot, 429-444.

Franke, Günter (1987b). Staatliche Risikozuweisung und Unternehmenspolitik. In: Henn, Rudolf (Hrsg.), Technologie, Wachstum und Beschäftigung, Festschrift für Lothar Späth. Berlin, Heidelberg: Springer, 808-821.

Franke, Günter (1989a). An Economic Analysis of Debt Equity Swaps. In: Vosgerau, Hans-Jürgen (ed.). New Institutional Arrangements for the World Economy. Studies in International Economics and Institutions. Berlin, Heidelberg: Springer, 213-233.

Franke, Günter (1989b). Institutionelle Gestaltungsmöglichkeiten zur Erleichterung des LDC-Portfeuille-Managements der Gläubigerbanken. In: Bombach, Gottfried, Bernhard Gahlen und Alfred E. Ott (Hrsg.). Die nationale und internationale Schuldenproblematik. Schriftenreihe des wirtschaftswissenschaftlichen Seminars Ottobeuren, Bd. 18. Tübingen: J.C.B. Mohr (Paul Siebeck), 137-160.

Franke, Günter (1990). Avenues for the Reduction of LDC-Debt - An Institutional Analysis. Universität Konstanz, Sonderforschungsbereich 178 "Internationalisierung der Wirtschaft", Diskussionsbeiträge, Serie II, Nr. 100.

Franke, Günter und Herbert **Hax** (1988). Finanzwirtschaft des Unternehmens und Kapitalmarkt. Berlin: Springer.

Frankfurter Allgemeine Zeitung "**FAZ**" (1. August 1989). Schuldenabbau soll Schutz der tropischen Regenwälder dienen. Nr. 175, 10.

Frankfurter Allgemeine Zeitung "**FAZ**" (6. Dezember 1986). Mehr Brasilianer fordern Schuldenboykott. Nr. 283, 13.

Frankfurter Allgemeine Zeitung "**FAZ**" (19. Februar 1988). Moody's stuft Banken zurück. Nr. 42, 13.

Frankfurter Allgemeine Zeitung "**FAZ**" (21. März 1988). Ohne Schmiergeld geht in Indonesien so gut wie nichts. Nr. 68, 14.

Frankfurter Allgemeine Zeitung "**FAZ**" (14. Juni 1989). Argentinienkredite abschreiben. Nr. 135, 23.

Friesen, Conny M. (1986). International Bank Supervision. London: Euromoney.

Furubotn, Eirik G. and Svetozar **Pejovich** (eds.) (1974). The Economics of Property Rights. Cambridge, MA.: Ballinger.

Furubotn, Eirik G. and Svetozar **Pejovich** (1974). Introduction: The New Property Rights Literature In: Furubotn, Eirik G. and Svetozar Pejovich (eds.). The Economics of Property Rights. Cambridge, MA.: Ballinger, 1-9.

Gäfgen, Gérard (1984). Entwicklung und Stand der Theorie der Property Rights: Eine kritische Bestandsaufnahme. In: Neumann, Manfred (Hrsg.). Ansprüche, Eigentums- und Verfügungsrechte. Arbeitstagung des Vereins für Socialpolitik, Gesellschaft für Wirtschafts- und Sozialwissenschaften in Basel 1983. Schriften des Vereins für Socialpolitik, Gesellschaft für Wirtschafts- und Sozialwissenschaften, Neue Folge, Bd. 140. Berlin: Duncker & Humblot, 43-62.

Gilbert, Nick (1986). Sheiks' Oil Puts the Skids Under US Rescue Plan. *Euromoney*, March, 45-55.

Gisselquist, David (1981). The Political Economy of International Bank Lending. New York: Praeger.

Glick, Reuven (1986). Economic Perspectives on Foreign Borrowing and Debt Repudiation: An Analytic Literature Review. Salomon Brothers Center for the Study of Financial Institutions. Monograph Series in Finance and Economics, No. 4. New York.

Goldberg, Ellen S. and Dan **Haendel** (1987). On Edge. International Banking and Country Risk. New York: Praeger.

Griffith-Jones, Stephany (1988). Debt Crisis Management, an Analytical Framework. In: Griffith-Jones, Stephany (ed.). Managing World Debt. Wheatsheaf: Harvester, 1-39.

Gruson, Michael (1988). Investment in Foreign Equity Securities and Debt-Equity Conversion by U.S. Banks, Bank Holding Companies, and Foreign Bank Holding Companies. *Columbia Business Law Review*, 2, 441-504.

Guttentag, Jack M. and Richard **Herring** (1986a). Disclosure Policy and International Banking. *Journal of Banking and Finance*, Vol. 10, No. 1, 75-97.

Guttentag, Jack M. and Richard **Herring** (1986b). Financial Innovations to Stabilize Credit Flows to Developing Countries. *Studies in Banking and Finance*, Vol. 3, 263-304.

Guttentag, Jack M. and Richard **Herring** (1987). Emergency liquidity assistance for international banks. In: Portes, Richard and Swoboda, Alexander K. (eds.). Threats to International Financial Stability. Cambridge: Cambridge University Press, 150-186.

Guttentag, Jack M. and Richard **Herring** (1989). Accounting for Losses on Sovereign Debt: Implications for New Lending. *Essays in International Finance*, No. 172, May, International Finance Section, Department of Economics, Princeton University. Princeton, N.J.

Gwynne, S.C. (1983). Adventures in the Loan Trade. *Harper's*, September, 22-26.

Hakim, Jonathan (1985). Latin America's Financial Crisis: Causes and Cures. In: Durán, Esperanza (ed.). Latin America and the World Recession. Published in association with The Royal Institute of International Affairs. Cambridge: Cambridge University Press, 17-37.

Hanley, Thomas H. **et al.** (1989). The Brady Plan - The Possible Implications of FASB 15. *Salomon Brothers Stock Research*, Commercial Banks, April 21, New York.

Hansen, Stein (1989). Debt for Nature Swaps - Overview and Discussion of Key Issues. *Ecological Economics*, 1, 77-93.

Hayek, Friedrich A. von (1973). Law, Legislation and Liberty. Vol. 1: Rules and Order. A new statement of the liberal principles of justice and political economy. Chicago: University of Chicago Press.

Hennart, Jean-François (1989). Can the "New Forms of Investment" Substitute for the "Old Forms"? A Transaction Costs Perspective. *Journal of International Business Studies*, Vol. XX, 2, Summer, 211-234.

Herrhausen, Alfred (1971). Zielvorstellungen und Gestaltungsmöglichkeiten einer Langfristplanung in Kreditinstituten. *Bank-Betrieb*, 10, 354-359

Hill, Wilhelm, Raymond **Fehlbaum** und Peter **Ulrich** (1974). Organisationslehre, Bd. 1. Ziele, Instrumente und Bedingungen der Organisation sozialer Systeme. Bern: Paul Haupt.

Holtz, Uwe (1988). Einleitung: Verschuldungskrise der Entwicklungsländer. In: Holtz, Uwe (Hrsg.). Verschuldungskrise der Entwicklungsländer. Anhörung im Deutschen Bundestag, Positionen der Fraktionen. Baden-Baden: Nomos, 7-27.

Holzmann, Oscar J. (1989). The Accounting Barrier to Foreign Debt/Equity Swaps. *International Business and Banking Discussion Papers*, No. 89-4, June, University of Miami.

Horn, Norbert (1984). Rechtsfragen internationaler Umschuldungen. *Wertpapiermitteilungen*, 22, 2. Juni, 713-721.

Hughes, Martin and Robert **Palache** (1984). Loan participations - some English law considerations, *International Financial Law Review*, November, 21-27.

Huizinga, Harry (1989). The Commercial Bank Claims on Developing Countries: How Have Banks Been Affected? In: Husain, Ishrat and Ishac Diwan (ed.). Dealing With the Debt Crisis. Washington, D.C.: The World Bank, 129-143.

Hurlock, James (1985). Debt Restructure Agreements: Perspective of Counsel for Borrowing Countries. In: Eskridge, William N. Jr. (ed). A Dance Along the Precipice. The Political and Economic Dimensions of the International Debt Problem. Lexington, MA.: Lexington Books, 119-134.

Hyde, Terrill A. (1988). U.S. Taxes: The Issues. In: Debt for Nature. An Opportunity. Information packet prepared by the National Wildlife Foundation and the World Wildlife Fund. Washington, D.C.

IMF Survey (1989). Paris Club Implements Menu Approach for Low-Income Countries. April 3, 103-104.

Institute of International Finance "**IIF**" (1987). Restoring Market Access. New Directions in Bank Lending. A Report by the Board of Directors. Washington, D.C.

International Monetary Fund "**IMF**" (1989). International Capital Markets. Developments and Prospects. World Economic and Financial Surveys, April, Washington, D.C.

Islam, Shafiqul (1989). Going Beyond the Brady Plan. *Challenge*, July-August, 39-46.

Jain, Arvind K. and Douglas **Nigh** (1989). Politics and the International Lending Decisions of Banks. *Journal of International Business Studies*, Vol. XX, 2, Summer, 349-359.

Jain, Arvind K. and Satyadev **Gupta** (1987). Some Evidence on "Herding" Behavior of U.S. Banks. *Journal of Money Credit, and Banking*, Vol. 19, 1, 78-89.

Jensen, Michael C. and William H. **Meckling** (1976). Theory of the Firm: Managerial Behavior, Agency Costs and Ownership Structure. *Journal of Financial Economics*, Vol. 3, 305-360.

Jung, Michael und Klaus **Spremann** (1989). Transaktionsrisiken. *Zeitschrift für Betriebswirtschaft*, 59. Jg., 1, 94-112.

Kahler, Miles (1986). Politics and international debt: explaining the crisis. In: Kahler, Miles (ed.). The Politics of International Debt. Ithaca: Cornell University Press.

Kaletsky, Anatole (1985). The Costs of Default. A Twentieth Century Fund Paper. New York: Priority Press.

Kieser, Alfred (1988). Erklären die Theorie der Verfügungsrechte und der Transaktionskostenansatz historischen Wandel von Institutionen? In: Budäus, Dietrich, Elmar Gerum und Gebhard Zimmermann (Hrsg.). Betriebswirtschaftslehre und Theorie der Verfügungsrechte. Wiesbaden: Gabler, 299-323.

Kreile, Michael (1987). Internationale Finanzmärkte und nationalstaatliche Außenpolitik. *Gegenwartskunde*, 2, 185-196.

Krugman, Paul R. (1989). Market-based Approaches to Debt Relief. In: Dornbusch, Rüdiger, John H. Makin and David Zlowe (eds.). Alternative Solutions to Developing-Country Debt Problems. Washington, D.C.: American Enterprise Institute for Public Policy Research, 43-63.

Kugler, Jacek (1987). The Politics of Foreign Debt in Latin America - A Study of the Debtors' Cartel. *International Interactions*, Vol. 13, 2, 115-144.

Lascelles, David (1988). Bankers stand by principle that loans must be repaid. *Financial Times*, March 15, 6.

Legg, Paul (1985). West Germany's Detente Policy Boomerangs. *The Wall Street Journal*, September 11, 33.

Lerbinger, Paul (1987). Finanzinnovationen und Schuldenkrise. *Die Bank*, 11, 594-601.

Lessard, Donald (1983). North-South. The Implications for Multinational Banking. *Journal of Banking and Finance*, 7, 521-536.

Lessard, Donald R. (1989). Country Risk and the Structure of International Financial Intermediation. In: Stone, Courtenay C. (ed.). Financial Risk: Theory, Evidence and Implications. Proceedings of the Eleventh Annual Economic Policy Conference of the Federal Reserve Bank of St. Louis. Boston: Kluwer Academic Publishers, 197-227.

Lichtenstein, Cynthia C. (1985). U.S. Response to the International Debt Crisis: The International Lending Supervision Act of 1983 and the Regulations Issued under the Act. In: Eskridge, William N. Jr. (ed). A Dance Along the Precipice. The Political and Economic Dimensions of the International Debt Problem. Lexington, MA.: Lexington Books, 177-206.

Link, Troland S. (1984). The Value of Bank Assets Subject to Transfer Risk. *Columbia Journal of Transnational Law*, 23:75, 75-82.

Lissakers, Karen (1984). Bank Regulation and International Debt. In: Feinberg, Richard E. and Valeriana Kallab (eds.). Uncertain Future: Commercial Banks and the Third World. U.S.-Third World Policy Perspectives, No. 2. Washington, D.C.: Overseas Development Council, 45-68.

Luckey, Eberhard-Rainer (1987). Bewertung von Länderrisiken in der Bankbilanz. In: Krumnow, Jürgen und Matthias. Metz (Hrsg.). Rechnungswesen im Dienste der Bankpolitik. Stuttgart: C.E. Poeschel, 287-296.

Makus, Klaus-Dieter (1986). Auslandsfilialen westdeutscher Geschäftsbanken in betriebswirtschaftlicher Sicht. Diss. Göttingen.

McDonald, Robert P. (1982). International Syndicated Loans. London: Euromoney.

McLure, Charles E., Jr. (1988). U.S. Tax Laws and Capital Flight from Latin America. *NBER Working Paper Series*, No. 2687, August. Cambridge, MA: NBER.

Mendelowitz, Alan I. (1987). Legislative and Administrative Obstacles to Writedowns and Swapping of Less Developed Country Debt. Statement before the Subcommittee on International Finance and Monetary Policy, Committee on Banking, Finance and Urban Affairs, United States Senate, April 2, United States General Accounting Office, Testimony. Unpublished.

Mendelowitz, Alan I. (1989). Federal Supervision of Overseas Lending By U.S. Banks. Statement before the Subcommittee on International Development, Finance and Monetary Policy, Committee on Banking, Finance and Urban Affairs, U.S. House of Representatives, June 27, United States General Accounting Office, Testimony. Unpublished.

Messer, Ulrich (1989). Rechtliche Rahmenbedingungen für die Betätigung von Geschäftsbanken im internationalen Forderungshandel. Schriften zum Internationalen Wirtschafts-, Finanz- und Steuerrecht, Bd. 1. Konstanz: Hartung-Gorre.

Michaelis, Elke (1985). Organisation unternehmerischer Aufgaben - Transaktionskosten als Beurteilungskriterium. Betriebswirtschaftliche Studien, Rechnungs- und Finanzwesen, Organisation und Institution, Bd. 4. Frankfurt am Main: Peter Lang.

Miller, Merton H. (1986). Financial Innovation: The Last Twenty Years and the Next. *Journal of Financial and Quantitative Analysis*, Vol. 21, 4, December. 459-471.

Morgan Guaranty Trust Company of New York (1984). Currency diversification for LDC external debt. *World Financial Markets*, August, 1-6.

Morgan Guaranty Trust Company of New York (1986). LDC capital flight. *World Financial Markets*, March, 13-15.

Morgan Guaranty Trust Company of New York (1987). LDC debt realities. *World Financial Markets*, June/July, 1-11.

Morgan Guaranty Trust Company of New York (1988). LDC debt reduction: a critical appraisal. *World Financial Markets*, issue 7, December 30, 1-12.

Morgan Guaranty Trust Company of New York (1989). Foreign Direct Investment in the United States. *World Financial Markets*, issue 2, June 29, 1-11.

Mudge, Alfred (1985). Sovereign Debt Restructuring: A Perspective of Counsel to Agent Banks, Bank Advisory Groups, and Servicing Banks. In: Eskridge, William N. Jr. (ed). A Dance Along the Precipice. The Political and Economic Dimensions of the International Debt Problem. Lexington, MA.: Lexington Books, 105-118.

Neue Züricher Zeitung "**NZZ**" (1989). US-Strafgesetze zur Förderung des Brady-Plans. Nr. 148, 30. Juni 1989, 13.

Nicolaides, C.M. (1987). Documentation of LDC Asset Transfers. *Butterworths Journal of International Banking and Financial Law*, August, 108-117.

Oberndörfer, Dieter (1989). Schutz der tropischen Regenwälder durch Entschuldung. Perspektiven und Orientierungen, Schriftenreihe des Bundeskanzleramtes, Bd. 5. München: C.H. Beck.

OECD (1987). Prudential Supervision in Banking. Paris.

Office of the Comptroller of the Currency, Board of Governors of the Federal Reserve System and Federal Deposit Insurance Corporation "**OCC/FRB/FDIC**" (1989a). Study on Accounting and Regulatory Policies Affecting Debt Restructuring. Washington, D.C.

Office of the Comptroller of the Currency, Board of Governors of the Federal Reserve System and Federal Deposit Insurance Corporation "**OCC/FRB/FDIC**" (1989b). Study on the Risks to the U.S. Banking System Posed by Troubled Foreign Loans. March 31, Washington, D.C.

Ongman, Joanne P.S. (1985). Federal Regulation of Lending Abroad: Past History, Current Practice, and Future Prospects. *Law and Policy in International Business*, Vol. 17, 679-719.

Park, Yoon S. and Jack **Zwick** (1985). International Banking in Theory and Practice. Reading, MA.: Addison -Wesley.

Peat Marwick (1986). Allowances for sovereign risk - an international survey. 2nd ed. Frankfurt.

Pine, Art (1986). Peru's Debt Defiance is Growing Difficult. *Wall Street Journal*, March 24.

Rauscher, Michael (1989). Foreign Debt and Renewable Resources. *Metroeconomica*, Vol. 40, 1, 57-66.

Reisner, Ralph, Michael **Gruson** and Roger W. **Thomas** (1988). Foreword. *University of Illinois Law Review*, 2, 219-224.

Roberts, David L. and Eli M. **Remolona** (1987). Debt Swaps: A Technique in Developing Country Finance. In: Rubin, Steven M. Guide to Debt Equity Swaps, Special Report No. 1104, September. London: The Economist Publications, 41-53.

Röller, Wolfgang (1987). Die Auslandsverschuldung Lateinamerikas. Ihre Ursachen, Probleme und mögliche Lösungen. Eichstätter Hochschulreden, Nr. 58. München: Minerva.

Roth, Thomas (1989). Bankenfonds für Debt Equity Swaps - rechtliche Grundlagen und praktische Ausgestaltung, dargestellt am Beispiel der Philippinen. konstanzer schriften zur rechtswissenschaft, Bd. 9. Dissertation. Konstanz: Hartung-Gorre.

Routledge, Nick (1985). Rescheduling, the Start of the Long, Long trail. *Euromoney*, March, 164-169.

Rowe, Nicholas (1989). Rules and Institutions. New York: Philip Allan.

Rubin, Steven M. (1987). Guide to Debt Equity Swaps, Special Report No. 1104, September. London: The Economist Publications.

Rubinstein, Javier H. (1988). The Federal Reserve Board's "Liberalization" of Restrictions on LDC Debt-Equity Swaps. *Law and Policy in International Business*, Vol. 20, 1, 163-180.

Sachs, Jeffrey D. (1989a). Introduction. In: Sachs, Jeffrey D. (ed.). Developing Country Debt and Economic Performance. Vol. 1, The International Financial System. Chikago: The University of Chikago Press, 1-35.

Sachs, Jeffrey D. (1989b). Making the Brady Plan Work. *Foreign Affairs*, Vol. 68, 3, 87-104.

Sachs, Jeffrey D. (1989c). Efficient Debt Reduction In: Husain, Ishrat and Ishac Diwan (ed.). Dealing With the Debt Crisis. Washington, D.C.: The World Bank, 239-257.

Sälter, Peter Michael (1989). Externe Effekte: "Marktversagen" oder Systemmerkmal? Wirtschaftswissenschaftliche Beiträge, Bd. 10. Heidelberg: Physica.

Salom, Ramón Escovar (1985). Venezuela: The Oil Boom and the Debt Crisis. In: Durán, Esperanza (ed.). Latin America and the World Recession. Published in association with The Royal Institute of International Affairs. Cambridge: Cambridge University Press, 120-127.

Sampson, Anthony (1982). The Money Lenders. Bankers in a Dangerous World. Sevenoaks: Hodder and Stoughton, Coronet Books.

Saunders, Anthony (1986). The Determinants of Country Risk. A Selective Survey of the Literature. *Studies in Banking and Finance*, 3, 1-38.

Saunders, Laura (1989). An offer they can't refuse. *Forbes*, May 29, 144.

Schroeder, R. Harold, Jr. and Robert W. **Swegle**, Jr.(1987). United States. In: Ernst & Whinney (ed.). International Bank Accounting. 2nd ed. London: Euromoney, 37-78.

Schubert, Martin W. (1987). Third World Debt as a Trading and Investment Tool. *Countertrade & Barter*, April/May, 38-43.

Schwarz, J. Adam (1987). Regulating the Loan Market for Developing Country Debt. In: Calverley, John and Richard O'Brien (eds.). Finance and the International Economy. The AMEX Bank Review Prize Essays. In memory of Robert Marjolin. Oxford: Oxford University Press. 84-97.

Sen, Amartya (1987). On Ethics and Economics. Oxford: Basil Blackwell.

Sidler, Eric F. (1983). Marketing Strategies in International Banking. In: Deutsches Komitee der AIESEC e.V./Walter Berger (Hrsg.). Why Go International? Lectures, Input Papers and Working Group Reports delivered at the VII. International Banking Seminar of AIESEC Germany, held at the Akademie der Volksbanken und Raiffeisenbanken, Schloß Montabaur, December 13-17, 1982. Frankfurt am Main: Fritz Knapp Verlag, 141-153.

Simon, Herbert A. (1976). Administrative Behavior. A Study of Decision Making Processes in Administrative Organization. 3rd ed., With New Introduction. New York: The Free Press.

Sinkey, Joseph F.,Jr. (1983). Commercial Bank Financial Management. New York: Macmillan.

Solo, Robert A. (1967). Economic Organizations and Social Systems. Indianapolis: Bobbs-Merrill.

Spindler, J. Andrew (1984). The Politics of International Credit. Private Finance and Foreign Policy in Germany and Japan. Washington, D.C.: The Brookings Institution.

Stannigel, Hellmut (1989). Pauschalwertberichtigungen auf Forderungen. *Zeitschrift für das gesamte Kreditwesen*, 6, 260-265.

Stausberg, Hildegard (1988). Mexiko ist mit seiner Umschuldungsaktion alles andere als zufrieden. *Frankfurter Allgemeine Zeitung*, Nr. 135, 7. März, 14.

Stein, Johann Heinrich von (1989). Internationales(n) Bankgeschäft, Innovationen im. In: Macharzina, Klaus und Martin K. Welge (Hrsg.). Handwörterbuch Export und Internationale Unternehmung. Stuttgart: Poeschel, 892-903.

Stokes, Bruce (1985). Mystery Surrounds Agenda, Decisions Of Foreign Loan Review Committee. *National Journal*, 9/21, 2136-2139.

Swoboda, Alexander K. (1985). Debt and the Efficiency and Stability of the International Financial System. In: Smith, Gordon W. and John T. Cuddington (eds.). International Debt and the Developing Countries. Washington, D.C.: The World Bank, 151-175.

Tajfel, Henri (1982). Gruppenkonflikt und Vorurteil. Entstehung und Funktion sozialer Stereotypen. Mit einem Vorwort von Wolfgang Stroebe. Bern: Verlag Hans Huber. English original: (1981). Human Groups and social categories. Studies in social Psycholgy. Cambridge: Cambridge University Press.

Taylor, Lance (1985). The Theory and Practice of Developing Country Debt: An Informal Guide for the Perplexed. *Journal of Development Planning*, 16, 195-227.

Touche Ross (1989). The Management of Corporate Taxes. London: Euromoney.

Treitel, Guenter H. (1987). The Law of Contract. 7. ed., London: Stevens & Sons.

Truell, Peter (1990). Mexico, Banks Reach Accord On Debt Load. *Wall Street Journal Europe*, Vol. VII, No. 240, January 12-13, 9.

Ulrich, Peter (1986). Transformation der ökonomischen Vernunft. Fortschrittsperspektiven der modernen Industriegesellschaft. 2., durchges. Aufl. 1987. Bern: Verlag Paul Haupt.

United Nations (1981). Transnational Banks: Operations, Strategies and their Effects in Developing Countries. New York: United Nations Centre on Transnational Coporations.

United Nations Centre on Transnational Corporations "**UNCTC**" (1983). Issues in Negotiating International Loan Agreements with Transnational Banks. New York: United Nations.

United States General Accounting Office "**GAO**" (1988). International Banking. Supervision of Overseas Lending Is Inadequate. Report to Congressional Requesters, May. Washington, D.C.

U.S. Accounting: A Summary (1988). In: Debt for Nature. An Opportunity. Information packet prepared by the National Wildlife Foundation and the World Wildlife Fund. Washington, D.C.

Vanberg, Victor (1983). Der individualistische Ansatz zu einer Theorie der Entstehung und Entwicklung von Institutionen. In Boettcher, E. et al. (eds.). Jahrbuch für Neue Politische Ökonomie, 2. Bd. Tübingen: Mohr-Siebeck. 50-69.

Wall Street Journal (1986). World Bank Clears Loans of $ 465 Million For Mexico Projects. March 27.

Walter, Ingo (1981). Country Risk, Portfolio Decisions and Regulation in International Bank Lending. *Journal of Banking and Finance*, 5, 77-92.

Watson, Maxwell **et al.** (1986). International Capital Markets. Developments and Prospects. World Economic and Financial Surveys, December, Washington, D.C.: International Monetary Fund.

Wellons, Philip (1985). Business-Government Relations in International Bank Lending: The Debt Crisis. In: Eskridge, William N. Jr. (ed). A Dance Along the Precipice. The Political and Economic Dimensions of the International Debt Problem. Lexington, MA.: Lexington Books, 135-150.

Williamson, John (1988). Voluntary Approaches to Debt Relief. Policy Analyses in International Economics, 25, September. Institute for International Economics, Washington, D.C.

Williamson, John and Donald R. **Lessard**. (1987). Capital Flight: The Problem and Policy Responses. Policy Analyses in International Economics, 23, November. Institute for International Economics, Washington, D.C.

Williamson, Mary L. (1988). The Role of Banking Regulation in Third World Debt Strategies. ODC working paper, May, Washington, D.C.: Overseas Development Council.

Williamson, Oliver E. (1979). Transaction-cost economics: The governance of contractual relations. *Journal of Law and Economics*, 22, 3-61.

Williamson, Oliver E. (1985). The Economic Institutions of Capitalism. Firms, Markets, Relational Contracting. New York: The Free Press.

Williamson, Oliver E. (1988). Corporate Finance and Corporate Governance. *Journal of Finance*, Vol. XLIII, 3, 567-591.

Witcher, S. Karene (1985). Latin American Debtors Display an Unusual Degree of Agreement. *Wall Street Journal*, December 23.

Witcher, S. Karene (1986). Mexico's Silva Herzog Campaigns For New Ways to Get Debt Relief. *Wall Street Journal*, March 26.

Wood, Philip (1984). Selected Aspects of International Loan Documentation and Rescheduling. In: Kalderen, Lars and Qamar S. Siddiqi in cooperation with Francis Chrommel and Patricia Watson (eds.). Sovereign Borrowers, Guidelines on Legal Negotiations with Commercial Lenders. Butterworths: Dag Hammarskjoeld Foundation, 123-143.

World Bank (1989a). The Tax, Accounting, and Regulatory Treatment of Sovereign Debt. Staff Working Paper. Cofinancing and Financial Advisory Services Department. Washington, D.C.

World Bank (1989b). World Debt Tables 1989-90. External Debt of Developing Countries. Vol. 1. Analysis and Summary Tables. Washington, D.C.

Wulfken, Jörg (1989). Juristische Strukturen und ökonomische Wirkungen von debt equity swaps. konstanzer schriften zur rechtswissenschaft, Bd. 13. Dissertation. Konstanz: Hartung-Gorre.

Wulfken, Jörg und Walter **Berger** (1988a). Internationaler Forderungshandel vor dem Hintergrund der Verschuldungskrise. *Recht der Internationalen Wirtschaft*, 8, 585-588.

Wulfken, Jörg und Walter **Berger** (1988b). Juristische und ökonomische Grundlagen des internationalen Handels von Kreditforderungen. *Zeitschrift für Vergleichende Rechtswissenschaft*, 335-375.

Yianni, Andrew and Chris **Oakley** (1987). Using negotiable securities in sovereign debt restructurings. *International Financial Law Review*, December, 37-40.

Young, John E. (1985). Supervision of Bank Foreign Lending. *Federal Reserve Bank of Kansas City Economic Review*, May, 31-39.

nbf neue betriebswirtschaftliche forschung

(Fortsetzung von S. II)

Band 28 Dr. Peter Wesner
Bilanzierungsgrundsätze in den USA

Band 29 Dr. Hans-Christian Riekhof
Unternehmensverfassung und Theorie der Verfügungsrechte

Band 30 Dr. Wilfried Hackmann
Verrechnungspreise für Sachleistungen im internationalen Konzern

Band 31 Prof. Dr. Günther Schanz
Betriebswirtschaftslehre und Nationalökonomie

Band 32 Dr. Karl-Heinz Sebastian
Werbewirkungsanalysen für neue Produkte

Band 33 Dr. Mark Ebers
Organisationskultur: Ein neues Forschungsprogramm?

Band 34 Dr. Axel v. Werder
Organisationsstruktur und Rechtsnorm

Band 35 Dr. Thomas Fischer
Entscheidungskriterien für Gläubiger

Band 36 Prof. Dr. Günter Müller-Stewens
Strategische Suchfeldanalyse

Band 37 Prof. Dr. Reinhard H. Schmidt
Modelle in der Betriebswirtschaftslehre

Band 38 Prof. Dr. Bernd Jahnke
Betriebliches Recycling

Band 39 Dr. Angela Müller
Produktionsplanung und Pufferbildung bei Werkstattfertigung

Band 40 Dr. Rudolf Münzinger
Bilanzrechtsprechung der Zivil- und Strafgerichte

Band 41 Dr. Annette Hackmann
Unternehmensbewertung und Rechtsprechung

Band 42 Dr. Kurt Vikas
Controlling im Dienstleistungsbereich mit Grenzplankostenrechnung

Band 43 Dr. Bernd Venohr
„Marktgesetze" und strategische Unternehmensführung

Band 44 Dr. Hans-Dieter Krönung
Kostenrechnung und Unsicherheit

Band 45 Dr. Theodor Weimer
Das Substitutionsgesetz der Organisation

Band 46 Dr. Hans-Joachim Böcking
Bilanzrechtstheorie und Verzinslichkeit

Band 47 Dr. Ulrich Frank
Expertenysteme: Neue Automatisierungspotentiale im Büro- und Verwaltungsbereich?

Band 48 Dr. Bernhard Heni
Konkursabwicklungsprüfung

Band 49 Dr. Rudolf Schmitz
Kapitaleigentum, Unternehmensführung und interne Organisation

Band 50 Dr. Ralf Michael Ebeling
Beteiligungsfinanzierung personenbezogener Unternehmungen. Aktien und Genußscheine

Band 51 Dr. Diana de Pay
Die Organisation von Innovationen. Ein transaktionskostentheoretischer Ansatz

Band 52 Dr. Michael Wehrheim
Die Betriebsaufspaltung in der Finanzrechtsprechung

Betriebswirtschaftlicher Verlag Dr. Th. Gabler GmbH, Postfach 15 46, 6200 Wiesbaden

GPSR Compliance

The European Union's (EU) General Product Safety Regulation (GPSR) is a set of rules that requires consumer products to be safe and our obligations to ensure this.

If you have any concerns about our products, you can contact us on ProductSafety@springernature.com

In case Publisher is established outside the EU, the EU authorized representative is:

Springer Nature Customer Service Center GmbH
Europaplatz 3
69115 Heidelberg, Germany

Batch number: 10726298

Printed by Printforce, the Netherlands